SHIPS &

DOCKS

ARCO PUBLISHING COMPANY, INC. New York

Edited by Donald Clarke

Published in 1978 by Arco Publishing Company, Inc.,
219 Park Avenue South, New York, NY 10003.

© Marshall Cavendish Limited 1978
All rights reserved

Printed in Great Britain

Library of Congress Cataloging in Publication Data

Main entry under title:

Ships and docks.

"This material has previously appeared in the
publication 'How it works'."
  1. Ships – Juvenile literature. I. Clarke,
Donald. II. Title.
VM150.S54   387.2   77-27628
ISBN 0-668-04556-6

INTRODUCTION

It seems clear that one area of science and technology that will never become obsolete or inefficient is that of *Ships and Docks*. Man's mastery of the sea was one of his earliest achievements, yet the most exciting aspect is that the power of the sea is never really mastered. And there will never be a substitute for leisurely travel or economical transport of goods on the water; even today the boat is the most prized possession of many a family.

In this book, *Ships and Docks*, every aspect of water transport is considered, from the simplest boat to the largest super-tanker. Canals, navigation, sailing techniques and many more subjects are expertly examined, with the help of excellent photographs and illustrations. And speaking of canals, it is easy to underestimate their importance – the English-speaking countries are the only industrialized countries which are not making efficient commercial use of their inland waterways. Did you know that a ton of goods can be shipped more than twenty times as far on the water for the same amount of money as by road haulage?

The waterways are there around the world, and they will be used as long as Man requires more than the bare minimum of subsistence. If civilization as we know it should end tomorrow, the technology of ships and docks is the first that would have to be rediscovered. It's all described in this book: *Ships and Docks*.

CONTENTS

SAFETY, SALVAGE AND ENGINEERING

INDEX

SAILING

A Badjan prahu with a Bugis praku behind.

The history of man's ability to keep himself and his goods afloat goes back many tens of thousands of years, and these earliest logs, bundles of reeds or branches, could travel only where water currents or primitive paddles allowed. After the discovery of paddles it would soon have become obvious that the wind could be as powerful an opponent to muscular propulsion as could be the currents and waves, thus frequently forcing an undesirable drift to leeward. That man fairly early learned to use this drift to advantage is clear from vase paintings and clay models of Egyptian origin, variously dated by archaeologists to be 7000 to 11,000 years old. Certainly by 3000 BC this controlled drifting, or downwind sailing, using large square-shaped sails was a firmly established seagoing technique for the transport of men and goods.

From the details of reliefs depicting these vessels we can deduce that the sails were hung from a horizontal spar (yard) which could be set at different angles to the wind by means of ropes attached to its ends. The square shape is obviously consistent with the earliest technologies of woven fibre or reed, it can be easily hung, raised or furled on to a simple spar, and when controlled by ties from its corners it is naturally blown by the wind into a near optimum curvature for downwind sailing, also allowing some angular variation from this course.

As in the much quicker development of modern fuel-driven transport devices, the technological development of sailing vessels has always been a com-

Compare these sail designs, the Indonesian prahu (below) and the felucca (left, on the Nile). The lateen on the felucca distorts if the wind is on the wrong side.

promise between demands for speed, cargo-carrying capacity and manoeuvrability, qualities which due to the complexity of their interaction and to local traditions and available materials throughout the world have led to the building of a tremendous variety of boats—by no means all successful.

The next important ability of a sailboat, after that of sailing fast downwind, is the ability to sail at angles departing from the downwind direction, and the greater this angle the greater will be the period of the voyage when wind can be used and oars put away. Thus an exceedingly important stage of this development is when a boat becomes capable of sailing reliably at 90° to the wind direction and so *holding station*. This achieved, the crew is completely independent of oars whatever the wind direction may be, as it is always possible to sail to any destination by holding station during periods of unfavourable winds, oars only being required for extreme wave-conditions and inshore navigation. Longer journeys would also become more acceptable as man's knowledge increased of the large scale circulations of wind over ocean surfaces, enabling routes to be picked which involved holding station for even less time. Easily established wind patterns, such

Left: the appearance of the Chinese junk has not changed for centuries, because it is very efficient. The battens in the sails maintain the shape even when sailing close to the wind.

as the monsoon in the Indian Ocean for example, might even eliminate the need for development of anything better than vessels that would just hold station, such as the *dhows* of the area.

Windward sailing

Gradually boats achieved the capability of sailing slightly into wind, a feature so contrary to intuition that it is not surprising that the associated technology seems to have been learned, lost and rediscovered many times and by many apparently well-separated societies, even though the ability itself might be considered to be the best method for its distribution. This only reflects the heavy overlay of tradition in sailing vessel construction. A success in some detail, once achieved, was held firmly in local collective memory to such an extent that it often inhibited, or made impossible, the incorporation of further improvements. The advantages of sailing closer into the eye of the wind are considerable; to be able to sail closer than a trading adversary often ensures the quickest delivery of cargo, or a wartime adversary can often be outmanoeuvred or eluded irrespective of his possible weapon superiority.

The way a sailing boat works is almost intuitive for downwind sailing. In common experience, any toy boat can be blown along irrespective of its shape of simple sail. It is sailing against the wind which needs explanation.

It is impossible for a boat with normal sails to sail directly into the wind. It is possible, however, to sail

Opposite page: the Polish ship Dar Pomarza *sails with the wind in the English Channel. 'Ship' here has a special meaning: ships are fully square rigged, with topmasts and topgallant masts.*
Above: the US Coastguard barque Eagle *is 'reaching' (sailing at an angle to the wind) during the 1972 Tall Ships race.*

along a line at right angles to the wind direction (*reaching*) by setting the sail closer to the centreline of the boat, rather than across it; it is easier for the boat to move through the water in the direction it is pointing, rather than sideways, so the result is that it moves at right angles to the wind. If the rudder is set so as to continually point the boat further into the wind, it is then possible to sail even closer to the wind direction. To progress into the wind, a series of paths at an angle to the wind are followed, first one way then the other, always getting a little further upwind. This procedure is called *beating*.

The special design features required for good windward sailing were only being realized in the 19th century and the racing yachts of today have windward performances well exceeding the fast clippers of the 1850 period, although their maximum speed when reaching at 90° to the wind is only slightly superior. These special features are those associated with sideforces at least as much as with the dragforces most important in downwind sailing.

Imagine a boat sailing close to the wind—that is, pointing to within about 45° of the wind direction. There are various forces on the sail and on the hull which can be split up into components in each direction. In each case, the sideforce is that force acting perpendicular to the flow of either air or water, and the dragforce is that acting along the flow. In each case these forces have a combined *resultant*. The sideforce on the sails and the sideforce on the hull act in roughly opposite directions because the wind is blowing on the sail, but the water is resisting the sideways movement of the hull.

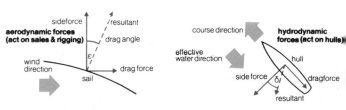

For successful sailing into the wind, the ratio of sideforces to dragforces must be a maximum, for both the aerodynamic forces acting on the sail rigging, and also for the hydrodynamic forces acting on the hull. That is, the sideforces should be as large as possible compared with their respective dragforces.

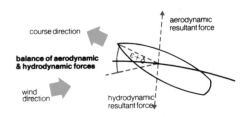

1 jigger topsail
2 spanker
3 mizzen royal
4 mizzen topgallant
5 mizzen upper topsail
6 mizzen lower topsail

7 mizzen crojack
8 mizzen topmast staysail
9 mizzen topgallant staysail
10 mainsail
11 main lower topsail
12 main upper topsail

13 main topgallant
14 main royal
15 main skysail
16 main royal staysail
17 main topgallant staysail
18 main topmast staysail

19 main staysail
20 foresail
21 fore lower topsail
22 fore upper topsail
23 fore topgallant
24 fore royal

25 fore skysail	31 fore topmast staysail	37 flying jib stay	43 skysail stay
26 upper studding sail	32 jib	38 flying jib stay	44 foot ropes
27 upper topsail studding sail	33 flying jib	39 fore royal stay	45 skysail braces
28 lower topsail studding sail	34 jib martingale	40 fore skysail stay	46 royal braces
29 lower studding sail	35 jib stay	41 fore skysail backstay	
30 fore staysail	36 flying jib martingale	42 fore royal backstay	

When a sailboat is in a steady sailing condition, the resultant aerodynamic forces must balance each other out completely. Therefore another way of stating the special conditions required for good windward sailing is that the drag angle of the sail (ε) and the drag angle of hull (δ) must each be as small as possible because, as the diagram shows, the angle of sailing into the wind is equal to the sum of ε and δ. As this sum decreases, so the boat will be capable of sailing closer into the wind.

The dragforce results from the fluid particles being slowed by the object itself, the drag being less as the shape is streamlined and its surface is smoothed. The sideforce (or lift in the case of aircraft) depends subtly on the curvature and thickness of the shape, which is similar to an aerofoil. The high values of sideforce coupled with low dragforce required by a sail for good windward performance demands thin spars and rigging, a stiff forward edge (luff) and a small curvature (camber) so that the shape is not destroyed when used at the low angles of wind incidence demanded for windward working. For hulls, good performance demands general smoothness, well-rounded bilges, deep keels, gentle stern exits from the water level, well-designed rudders and a low and smooth silhouette above water.

The origin of sideforce, at its simplest, is the Newtonian reaction to the deflection of fluid particles with greater momentum toward one side of the hull than to the other side due to the hull being aligned asymmetrically to the water flow. Bernoulli's equation, used in hydro- and aerodynamics, shows that the static pressure is lower on the side which has the higher water velocity past it. Thus a sail (or hull) is essentially sucked sideways by the leeside static pressure being lower than the mean value due to its higher streaming speed, assisted to a lesser degree by the excess pressure or slower streaming speed on the windward side.

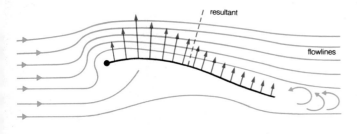

Finally, it should be noted that however small the drag angles can be made for sails and hulls, there will be no point if the opposing aerodynamic and hydrodynamic sideforces in practice cause such heeling of the vessel that the sideforce is seriously reduced. Therefore additional qualities required for windward performance are those associated with righting stability: low centre of gravity or deep heavy keels, lightweight superstructure coupled with high centre of buoyancy.

The particularly successful sailing vessels of the past can now be assessed in terms of these criteria for good windward performance. There is much evidence to suggest that the ability to hold station with the early square sail was first exhibited by the phenomenal North Atlantic voyages of the Norse longships of the 7th to 10th centuries. These ships, ranging in size from 70 to 270 feet (21 to 82 m) had hulls which even today are considered to have an excellent low drag profile, while the sail rigging exhibited for the first time special cordage (bowlines) and spars (beitass) so

Above: a Thames barge, using a bowsprit, which allows an extra foresail. Opposite page: the five-masted ship Preussen, *built in 1902. She was 407 feet long and 53 feet in beam.*

arranged as to tighten the luff and to ensure the sail remains correctly shaped at low angles of incidence.

Square sails can also be kept in shape at low incidence by incorporating stiff horizonal battens of bamboo, as in the early Chinese junks, which also had low silhouettes and good underwater characteristics, having developed the more efficient central rudder centuries before European vessels. These junks were so well developed by the 13th century, and bear such strong resemblance to the large ocean-going junks of today, that it is probable they were sailing well into the wind centuries earlier.

Sails in which the yard was used at such an angle to the mast that it acted as a stiff leading edge, the so-called lateen (after 'latin') sail, could be set close to the wind and so contributed much to the technique of windward sailing. Its earliest appearance in the ocean-going Polynesian sailing canoes of the 5th century, and especially in the Mediterranean from the 9th to 13th centuries, led to classes of boats whose high efficiency contributed much to the well-documented exploration and merchanting exploits of the Venetians and Portuguese caravels, continuing a chain of development which includes the Scandinavian 17th century jachts (present word yacht) and the famous Massachusetts schooners, which became the direct forerunners of the modern ocean-racer. In this development process, it seems probable that the lateen sail was split into two more manageable sails: the foresail whose leading edge was sharpened by replacing the oblique yard by a permanently set sail luff, and the aft or mainsail suspended on the aft portion of the yard which then became the gaff. This latter spar eventually disappeared when it became necessary to reduce topside weight and in the process left the modern Bermudan sail which exhibited windward advantages now ascribed to its height compared with its length, or aspect ratio.

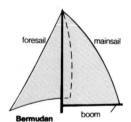
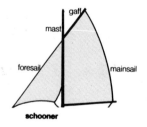

Developments of sailing vessels in this century are based on long experience, together with all the current scientific measuring and deductive techniques. Models of sails and rigging are tested in wind tunnels in the same way as aircraft models are tested, the major measurements being those of dragforce, sideforce and centre of effort (the point on which the combined effect of the sails and rigging can be said to act) as the speed and angle of incidence of the wind, and also sometimes

the heel angle of the sail are varied. The forces measured on the models by dynamometers are then scaled to predict the actual forces to be expected on a full-size rig. Similarly, models of hulls are towed to different speeds and attitudes in towing tanks and the dragforce, sideforce and centre of effort (in this case usually called centre of lateral resistance) acting on the model are measured and scaled to predict the actual forces expected on the full-size hull, Such measurements are most often used as comparisons to check possible advantages of small variations. Occasionally, model hull and sail measurements can be used together to predict the performance of designed but unbuilt boats, a process needing considerable engineering skill and large computer facilities.

It can be recognized, perhaps, that the many measurements required to completely predict an unbuilt yacht's performance requires the skills and instrumental resources of both aerodynamic and hydrodynamic laboratories and demand more actual measurements than required for an aircraft and ship together. It is not surprising, therefore, that such a full programme of measurement is rarely performed for an end product which is essentially recreational. More usually, yacht development arises from a mixture of limited wind tunnel and towing tank tests, together with experience of successful yachts and also trial and error with full-size new boats.

To improve the performance of a given boat, modern shipboard electronic instruments will provide the crew with instantaneous readings of windspeed, wind direction, waterspeed, course direction and even complicated combinations of these readings, the most useful for beating being the effective yachtspeed as if travelling directly into the eye of the wind (speed made good). Most sailors today, however, as throughout history, use their own experience or quite simple devices to estimate the same measurements in order to improve performance.

Sailing boats, as for all other technologies, have always advanced as a result of improvements in materials of construction. Sails need strong, light-weight, fairly stiff, smooth surfaced, bacterial and

*Left: a fore-and-aft rig
sailing close to the wind.
Below: modern lightweight
materials have taken some
of the hard work out of
sport sailing—but not
all of it.*

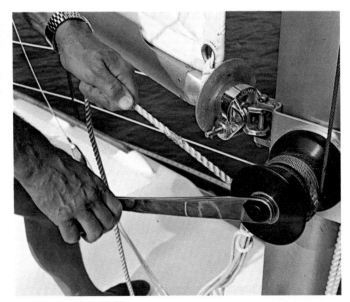

sunshine resistant fabrics with little mechanical fatigue or creep and which will not let the wind through. Vast improvements in most of these properties have been made by replacing natural fibres by woven and hot calendered (passed through hot rollers) synthetic fibres, particularly of the Terylene [Dacron] family, but there is still room for improvement. Rigging needs materials of high intrinsic tensile strength (strength for weight) and density, while spars need materials of high intrinsic stiffness together with high corrosion resistance. Hemp, then iron, then galvanized steel has been replaced by stainless steel rigging, while anodized aluminium alloy tubes, fibre or honeycomb composites now replace wooden spars. Hulls need corrosion resistant materials suitable for forming into smooth, lightweight skins of great strength and shock resistance and that most excellent material, wood, is being replaced particularly by aluminium alloys and fibre-reinforced plastics. Thus each new material is rapidly incorporated into designs as its cost allows.

BOATBUILDING

Thor Heyerdahl built boats to prove the viability of his theories of the travels of ancient peoples. This boat, made of papyrus after an Egyptian tomb drawing, sailed across the Atlantic.

Boats developed from a number of primitive water craft in different places and at different times. The earliest such craft may have been a log used as a float to cross a river. The log became a dug-out canoe when fire and axes were used to hollow it out. Two such canoes were lashed together for stability, or an outrigger was added. In pre-historic Europe, stability seems to have been achieved by placing weights in the bottom of the canoe.

In Egypt, where timber was not available, boats were built by lashing together bundles of reeds, and pulling the two ends of the boat up from the water by means of ropes. In China, flat bamboo rafts were in use for river haulage, probably from about 4000 BC. Later, perhaps about 1000 BC, they began to adapt these rafts by laying the bamboo along the curved sides of semi-circular wooden planks, thus creating a vessel which had a number of solid bulkheads down its length. This continued to be developed until it resulted in today's Chinese 'junk'. Another ancient type of boat, the wooden frame covered with skin or bark, survives today in the form of the Irish curragh, the Eskimo kayak and the American Indian canoe.

For thousands of years, wood was the most common material used in boatbuilding, but in the 1950s glass

Below: Lake Titicaca, in Peru. The traditional boat of the local fisherman is made of bundles of reeds lashed together, and is remarkably similar to ancient Egyptian boats.

reinforced plastic brought rapid changes, allowing mass production techniques and greater flexibility in hull design. Today about 70% of boats built in Europe and the USA are made of GRP.

Plank construction

Boatbuilding in wood is a skilled craft involving the use of a great many wooden components to build a watertight structure. This has to combine stability in the water with the ability to withstand stresses often comparable with those experienced by jet aircraft.

Wood boatbuilding follows two principal styles, clincher (sometimes spelled clinker) with overlapping planking, and carvel or caravel where the planking is smooth. The clincher or lapstrake technique gives a 'monocoque' or stressed skin construction. The shape

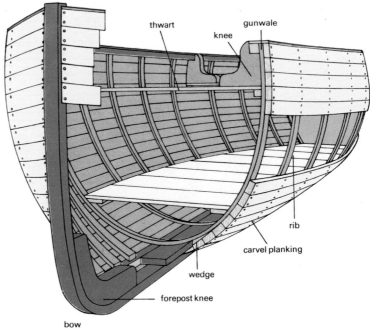

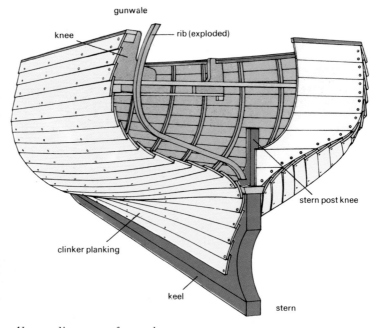

Above: diagrams of carvel (top) and clinker construction. In the carvel, the planks are fitted smoothly to the frame, usually from the top down. In the clinker, the planks are fitted from the keel up, overlapping each other, and the ribs are fitted afterwards.

21

of the craft is developed by the addition of successively fastened planks, sometimes using only a single mould or guidance shape amidships. After the planking is completed, light frames are steamed or sawn to shape and added to the interior to strap the planking together as a safeguard against a plank splitting along the grain. This construction makes the boat very light but vulnerable to damage. The overlapping edges or lands of the planking are liable to wear and it is difficult to keep the planking watertight once it has been disturbed. It is therefore normally used only for small craft such as beach boats.

In carvel construction wooden planks are fitted edge to edge over a completed framework which determines the shape and forms the structural support of the finished craft. The framework consists of a centreline piece called the keel with a companion piece called a keelson, a stem at the front which is joined to the keel with a wooden knee (angle piece) called a foregripe. At the other end the upright part of the framing consists of a sternpost with a supporting knee. The framing across the boat is normally built with timber sawn from branches whose grain lies roughly in the required curves. These frames are in turn strapped together inside with full length wooden planks called stringers, and at the deck edge with an inwale or interior plank which is sometimes called a beam shelf if it has to carry the deck beams. Originally a number of heavy planks called wales were arranged longitudinally and fastened to the outside of the frame before the skin planking was fitted. Their function was to stop the planking from spreading when the caulking compound was hammered between the planks to make the hull watertight. With modern improvements in building techniques, wales have largely disappeared.

There are many variants of the two techniques and light, steam-bent strap frames are often used to augment and lighten the sawn frame structure. Other common variations include composite constructions where steel frames are used with a wooden keel and planking; multiple planking, where two or more layers are placed diagonally to make a strong skin which is more watertight, though difficult to repair, and strip planking. Very narrow planks are used in the normal planking but are nail fastened through their thickness to the previous plank as well as being fastened to the frames.

To get the best performance from a fast power boat a knuckle or chine (projecting corner) must be built at the division between the bottom and sides of the hull. This chine is built like the centreline keel and the technique is known as a chine construction.

Plywood

During the 1920s boatbuilding techniques using plywood were developed, largely in the USA. The invention of waterproof resin adhesives led to the development of water resistant 'marine grade' plywood. This quickly became popular for building bulkheads or

vertical wall divisions of the hull and later it became a very common material for the planking skins of inexpensive small craft. This technique, still widely used in 'do it yourself' built craft, was the first real attempt to use glue to stop water from entering between the components of the hull.

Despite great ingenuity, the shapes which can be constructed from bending flat sheets of plywood are very limited and were invariably angular in appearance. The next step therefore was to make the actual plywood sheets over a curved mould of the required shape. This type of building is now used for high-quality racing yachts where the high costs involved can be balanced against the strength and light weight. This moulded plywood construction involves the planking of the mould with very thin wood sheets of veneer thickness. These are added in successive glued diagonal layers until a finished thickness approximately half that of a carvel planked hull is achieved. If cold setting adhesives are used each layer is held down with staples until the glue sets. For hot moulded construction the layers are held in place by air bags or a vacuum press and moved into an oven to give a quick 'cure' to the hot setting glue.

A variation of this construction is the use of laminated structural members. Here the keel, stem, beam, and ribs are built up over a mould to the required dimensions and curves.

Glass reinforced plastics

The most popular form of construction today uses polyester resin reinforced with glass fibre, generally spoken of as fibreglass or glass reinforced plastics (GRP). The normal building process starts with the construction of a full size solid model of the final boat, called the plug. Over this a hollow mould is formed by a similar process to the hull construction. The hull and deck mouldings, and even mouldings for the interior accommodation, are formed in separate moulds.

The materials used in GRP construction consist basically of polyester resin reinforced with finely spun glass fibres either in cut pieces or made up into a woven cloth.

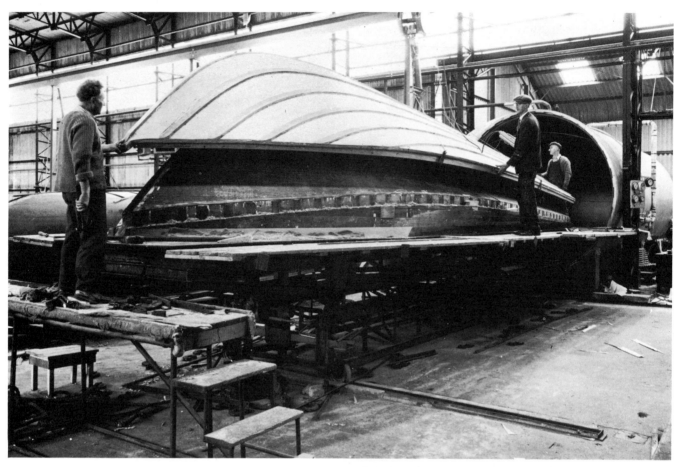

Above: the bottom hull section of a moulded plywood racing yacht after curing in an oven.
Below right: concrete boats are cheap and strong; they are popular in underdeveloped countries. Opposite page, top: a ship's hull of fibreglass.
Bottom:'plating' an aluminum racing yacht.

The mould is first coated with wax or some other release agent to prevent the resin from adhering to the surface. Next a gel or surface coat of resin, usually impregnated with pigment to suit the final colour scheme, is sprayed or painted onto the surface of the mould. A very light supporting mat of glass fibres is then placed on top of the resin and pressed in with a roller until completely saturated with wet resin. Subsequent layers of moulding resin with heavier glass reinforcement carefully rolled into it are added until the required hull thickness and strength are attained. The resin hardens in three stages: first to a soft gel, then to a point where the moulding can be removed from the mould, and then over a period of weeks it matures to full strength. Bulkheads and reinforcements are added to the moulding either in or just out of the mould. Considerable skill and care are necessary in glass fibre construction in order to make certain that the resin is properly supported by glass at all corners

and edges, that no air is trapped between the layers and that the glass is thoroughly saturated with resin.

Another common method of fibreglass construction uses a hand spray gun to deposit both the resin and chopped glass strands which leaves a mat of partly saturated fibre that must then be rolled to complete saturation as before. This method involves skilled spraying and accurate control of quantities to ensure uniformity. Glass fibre construction is also mechanized in other ways, such as the use of glass mats previously saturated with resin, and vacuum or pressure resin saturation of previously laid glass reinforcements.

The undoubted advantage of the glass reinforced plastics method of construction is the monocoque or stressed skin nature of the hull, without any joins where water might enter. Another benefit is the reduction of maintenance, which can be one tenth of that for a conventional wooden hull. Further benefits lie in being able to use the moulds for production building, and the ease of achieving a high finish. The material, however, is fairly heavy (flotation chambers are often included) and inconveniently flexible. One way of correcting these faults is a 'sandwich' construction where another material is placed between the GRP layers to improve stiffness and reduce weight. End grain balsa wood slabs or foam plastics are commonly used over areas or in patterns as required during the course of the hull moulding.

The cost of building a single hull in glass fibre is very high owing to the cost of the plug and mould. To overcome this some craft are built with a PVC or polyurethane foam core planked over moulds like a traditional wooden hull and then covered with fibreglass inside and out. The outside surface of the hull is ground, sanded smooth and paint finished.

Other plastics boatbuilding methods include simple foam plastic castings and vacuum forming, where a plastic sheet material such as ABS or polyethylene is heated until soft and then sucked down over a hull-shaped former. This is either thick enough and the right shape to be rigid in its own right, or it may be formed of two or more mouldings which are filled with injected foam to give buoyancy.

Other materials

Boats are also built in metal. Steel, for instance, has been a common material for building boats as well as ships. Its strength and weight characteristics limit its use to larger craft but with welded construction and the new anti-rust coating, steel has become more versatile.

Aluminium is also a popular material for high performance one-off yachts, increasingly since new alloys have reduced the original serious corrosion problems of aluminium in salt water. The metal's lightness also makes it suitable for small craft which have to be manhandled. Some small aluminium hulls are made by stretch forming, where a sheet of material is stretched bodily into shape over a hull-shaped former. 25

The Queen Mary, *one of the most famous of liners.*

SHIPS

In 2500 BC the Egyptians were building fairly sophisticated sailing vessels; from then until the 19th century, ships were built mostly of wood and powered by sails.

At the end of the 16th century, the French inventor Denis Papin outlined plans for a boat with revolving paddles powered by a simple steam engine. Early steam engines, however, were far too big and heavy to be installed in boats. In the middle of the 18th century, the trickle of ideas, drawings and patents began to turn into a flood and finally in 1783 a paddle steamer called *Pyroscaphe* steamed against the current of the River Saone in France for fifteen minutes.

Three years later a steamboat built by John Fitch was tested on the River Delaware in America, and there were other early experiments. The *Charlotte Dundas* is known as the first successful steamboat because she towed two loaded vessels along the Forth and Clyde canal in March 1803. This steamboat was inspected by Robert Fulton, an American inventor and painter, whose *Clermont* began carrying farepaying passengers on the Hudson River in New York State in September of the same year, making the steamboat a commercial success.

Today nearly all merchant ships and warships are built of metal and powered by Diesel engines or steam turbines. The way in which the vessel is constructed depends upon the type of ship and the technique adopted at the shipyard, and this will be influenced by the available yard machinery and cranes.

For example, a bulk carrier will usually be constructed in the following way by most shipyards. Firstly the bottom shell and longitudinals will be laid on the building berth as a single unit after manufacture in the assembly shed, then the double-bottom unit will be lowered on to the bottom shell and welded into position. The wing-tank unit is lifted into position, aligned and welded up, and a pair of bulkheads are erected the correct distance apart over the hold length, with an allowance made for their inclination to suit the declivity (downslope) of the building berth necessary for launching. A side-shell panel can then be connected to the lower wing-tank unit and bulkheads to form the sides of the hold. Then the upper wing-tank is lowered into place and welded with the remaining deck panel finally completing the amidship structure. The ship is also built forward and aft of midships simultaneously. This technique, although not adopted by every shipyard, does allow an even spread of labour force. Working from midships gives a good reference structure for taking dimensions during the building.

When each heavy unit is lifted on to the berth, the bottom of the vessel is checked for alignment by an optical system. Any distortion which may occur would affect the strength of the hull as well as hydrodynamic efficiency.

Right: Fulton's paddle steamer Clermont, *the first commercially successful steamboat.*

28

Above: Isambard Kingdom Brunel made revolutionary advances in railways, bridges and shipbuilding. Above left: the 19,000 ton Great Eastern *was a commercial failure, but laid the first submarine cable across the Atlantic.*

MERCHANT SHIPS

Dry-cargo vessels

The basic orthodox design for a dry cargo vessel consists of a double bottom, several holds, a midship engine room and a forward and after peak-tank. Usually they have one or two decks and three main superstructures. These superstructures are a forecastle, bridge and a poop located at the bow, the middle and the stern of the ship respectively, and they extend to the sides of the vessel. The ship is sub-divided with steel divisions called bulkheads, which are watertight from the bottom of the vessel up to the main strength deck. Their main function is to restrict flooding if the hull is damaged, but they also support the deck and prevent the hull from distorting because of cargo or sea pressure.

The double bottom is a safety device in case the bottom shell is damaged; it also provides a space for storage of fuel oil, water ballast or fresh water. The double-bottom structure gives great strength to the bottom of the ship, which is essential for dry-docking operations. The forward and after peak-tanks are normally exclusively used for water ballast to give adequate draught when the vessel is unloaded and to adjust the trim if necessary.

The forecastle tween decks (short for 'between') are used for bosun's stores, the storage of wire ropes and rigging equipment and for paint and lamps. On the forecastle deck, each anchor cable passes from the windlass down through a spurling pipe into the chain locker, where the ends of the cables are connected to

The diagrams on the right are examples of structural features of common types of merchant ships.
Opposite page: a supertanker constructed in a Japanese shipyard was too large to be launched normally, so it was built in a drydock which was flooded when the ship was ready. It has a capacity of 276,000 tons deadweight.

oil tanker midship section

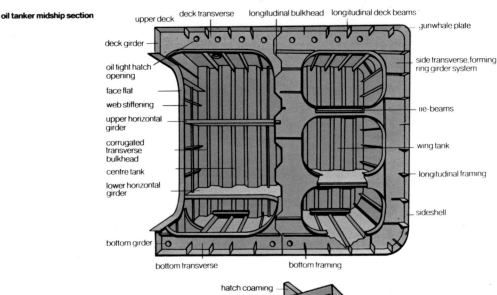

upper deck · deck transverse · longitudinal bulkhead · longitudinal deck beams · gunwhale plate · deck girder · oil tight hatch opening · face flat · web stiffening · upper horizontal girder · corrugated transverse bulkhead · centre tank · lower horizontal girder · side transverse, forming ring girder system · tie-beams · wing tank · longitudinal framing · sideshell · bottom girder · bottom transverse · bottom framing

bulk carrier

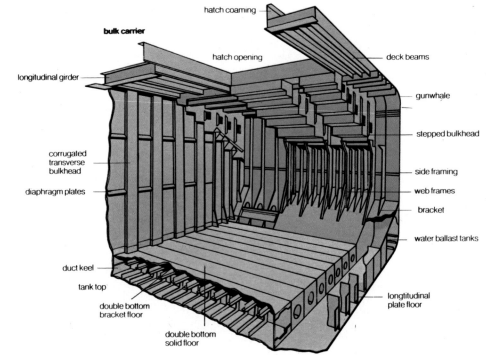

hatch coaming · longitudinal girder · hatch opening · deck beams · gunwhale · stepped bulkhead · corrugated transverse bulkhead · diaphragm plates · side framing · web frames · bracket · water ballast tanks · duct keel · tank top · longtitudinal plate floor · double bottom bracket floor · double bottom solid floor

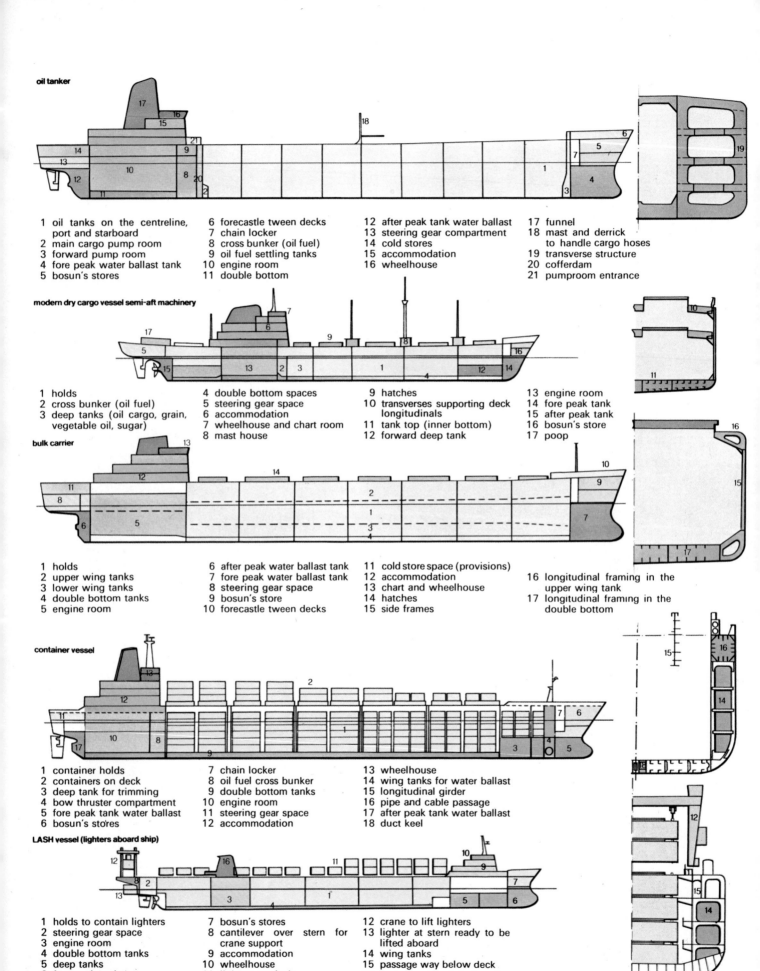

oil tanker

1 oil tanks on the centreline, port and starboard
2 main cargo pump room
3 forward pump room
4 fore peak water ballast tank
5 bosun's stores
6 forecastle tween decks
7 chain locker
8 cross bunker (oil fuel)
9 oil fuel settling tanks
10 engine room
11 double bottom
12 after peak tank water ballast
13 steering gear compartment
14 cold stores
15 accommodation
16 wheelhouse
17 funnel
18 mast and derrick to handle cargo hoses
19 transverse structure
20 cofferdam
21 pumproom entrance

modern dry cargo vessel semi-aft machinery

1 holds
2 cross bunker (oil fuel)
3 deep tanks (oil cargo, grain, vegetable oil, sugar)
4 double bottom spaces
5 steering gear space
6 accommodation
7 wheelhouse and chart room
8 mast house
9 hatches
10 transverses supporting deck longitudinals
11 tank top (inner bottom)
12 forward deep tank
13 engine room
14 fore peak tank
15 after peak tank
16 bosun's store
17 poop

bulk carrier

1 holds
2 upper wing tanks
3 lower wing tanks
4 double bottom tanks
5 engine room
6 after peak water ballast tank
7 fore peak water ballast tank
8 steering gear space
9 bosun's store
10 forecastle tween decks
11 cold store space (provisions)
12 accommodation
13 chart and wheelhouse
14 hatches
15 side frames
16 longitudinal framing in the upper wing tank
17 longitudinal framing in the double bottom

container vessel

1 container holds
2 containers on deck
3 deep tank for trimming
4 bow thruster compartment
5 fore peak tank water ballast
6 bosun's stores
7 chain locker
8 oil fuel cross bunker
9 double bottom tanks
10 engine room
11 steering gear space
12 accommodation
13 wheelhouse
14 wing tanks for water ballast
15 longitudinal girder
16 pipe and cable passage
17 after peak tank water ballast
18 duct keel

LASH vessel (lighters aboard ship)

1 holds to contain lighters
2 steering gear space
3 engine room
4 double bottom tanks
5 deep tanks
6 fore peak tanks
7 bosun's stores
8 cantilever over stern for crane support
9 accommodation
10 wheelhouse
11 lighters on deck
12 crane to lift lighters
13 lighter at stern ready to be lifted aboard
14 wing tanks
15 passage way below deck
16 funnel port and starboard

Below: preparing prefabricated steel sections in a Finnish shipyard.

the fore-peak bulkhead by a cable clench.

At the after end there is a steering gear compartment where a hydraulic mechanism is used to move the rudder. The control for the steering gear is transmitted from the wheelhouse by a telemotor system. Directly below the steering gear compartment is the rudder trunk which houses the upper rudder stock that is used to turn the rudder. The poop and bridge are used for accommodation and for provision stores, some of which may be refrigerated.

As diesel machinery is thermally more efficient than other types it is often used in dry-cargo vessels. The propeller is driven directly from a slow speed, in-line engine. The propeller shaft passes to the after end through a shaft tunnel; this tunnel protects the shaft from the cargo in the holds and it provides access for maintenance of the shaft and bearings.

In addition to the main engine, the engine room contains auxiliary machinery such as diesel generators, oil purifiers, air compressors, ballast and bilge pumps, cooling water pumps and many other essential items of equipment. Just forward of the engine room are the settling tanks, fuel oil bunkers and a deep tank port and starboard, which may be used to carry liquid cargoes or a dry cargo such as grain or sugar. The accommodation is practically all amidships with the officers berthed on the bridge deck or boat deck. The wheelhouse, chart-room and radio room are usually together and the captain may have his dayroom, bedroom, toilet and office on the same deck. Galleys, pantries, lavatories and recreation rooms are carefully positioned to control the noise level and prevent annoyance to the off-duty crew.

The latest dry-cargo vessels have the engine room nearer to the stern. This shortens the shaft length and leaves a clear deck space forward of the bridge in which to work the cargo. Many vessels now have deck cranes for cargo handling instead of derricks operated by winches, and some vessels are fitted with special heavy lifting equipment.

Bulk carriers

These are single-deck, single-screw vessels which carry large quantities of bulk cargo such as grain, sugar, bauxite and iron ore. The engines are installed at the after end to leave the better spaces in the hull for cargo and the accommodation is all aft above the engine room, so that services and sanitation are concentrated in one region of the vessel. Upper and lower wing-tanks extend over the whole length of the cargo holds and they are used for water ballast when the ship is in the unloaded or light condition to give sufficient draught to immerse the propeller and give a better control over the empty vessel in heavy seas. The slope of the upper wing-tank is designed to restrict the movement of a grain cargo, 33

which may otherwise cause the vessel to become unstable. The double-bottom tank is used for fuel oil or for water ballast, and these tanks can be used to make adjustments to the trim of the ship. Some bulk carriers have their own derricks or deck cranes, but many rely entirely on the dockside amenities for loading and discharging cargo. The hull construction of these vessels is a combination of two framing systems in order to obtain the best strength characteristics from each. The deck, wing-tanks and double bottom are longitudinally framed and the side shell is transversely framed.

Container ships

These vessels are a relatively new concept in cargo handling which reduces the time that the vessel stays in port. The containers also form a complete load for road vehicles without further handling. British built vessels are normally designed for 20 ft (6.1 m) long containers, but they can be modified for 40 ft (12.2 m) containers if necessary. The hold length is designed to suit the length and number of containers to be fitted into the hull, and to allow sufficient space for refrigeration coolers and coupling systems for these containers with perishable cargo. The accommodation and machinery on these vessels are usually located aft to leave a

Above: a large prefabricated section being lifted into place in a shipyard at Yokohama.
Next page: laying the wooden deck during construction of Cunard's liner Queen Elizabeth 2.

clear deck for cargo working and to allow the large crane an unrestricted region for operation. The shore container crane and its lifting spreader system will only lift standard containers and hatch lids with correctly designed corner fittings. All the holds have vertical guides to position the containers and give support, especially to the lowest container which could distort under the load transmitted down from those above. The containers are placed in a fore and aft attitude as the cargo experiences less ship motion in this direction, and when lifted ashore they are more readily received by road and rail transport. One advantage of container vessels is that they can carry containers on deck, but the number of tiers depends on the strength of the hatch lids and the necessity of having a clear view from the wheelhouse. The stability of a vessel with a deck cargo must always be checked, as the centre of mass of the vessel will be raised and it may cause the ship to roll or capsize. All deck containers are lashed to the hatches with steel rods or wires which have hooks and

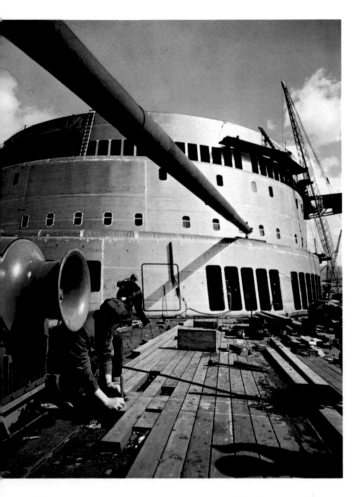

along the deck to the hold. Each lighter is handled in about 15 minutes, and at present the LASH vessel will carry about 80 lighters, each with a cargo capacity of approximately 400 tons, a length of 61 ft 6 in (18.8 m) and a width of 31 ft 2 in (9.5 m). As well as being stowed in the holds, lighters can also be stowed in tiers of two on top of the large single-piece pontoon-type hatch covers, which have metal fittings for keeping the lighters secure during heavy weather at sea. The crane is equipped with a hydraulically operated latching device to grip the lighters and hatch covers, and a swell compensator which holds the lighter steady at the stern irrespective of the relative movements of the ship and the lighter in the sea.

The advantages of the system are that cargo-handling operations can be carried out in parts of the world where large ships cannot be berthed as the depth of water is insufficient. Mixed cargoes can be handled simultaneously, and the lighters can be towed to various places up river after unloading, thus providing a virtual door-to-door service.

Passenger vessels

In recent years the number of very large passenger liners has diminished in favour of the smaller vessel, capable of being converted for winter cruising. The vessel will normally comply with the regulations of all maritime countries, including those of the US coastguard, allowing it to change to cruising at any time.

Passenger vessels are more comprehensively subdivided than other merchant ships so that, if several adjacent compartments are flooded, the ship will remain stable and stay afloat. If asymmetrical flooding occurs, the vessel has cross-flooding fittings to reduce the angle of heel.

Lifeboats are fitted port and starboard on the boat deck with sufficient capacity for the total number of passengers that the ship is certified to carry. Fire control is another important safety aspect, and the vessels are subdivided vertically into fire zones with steel bulkheads. In these zones the bulkheads must be capable of preventing the spread of a flame in a 30-minute standard fire test, and the accommodation must have an automatic fire alarm and detection system.

A gyroscopically controlled set of stabilizers or fins are a common feature on most passenger vessels, to control the amount of roll and give a more comfortable crossing. For manoeuvring, these vessels are often fitted with bow thrusters, and they usually have twin-screw main propulsion.

The better cabins are located on the higher decks and the one, two or three-berth ordinary cabins on the lower decks. One of the most important areas in the accommodation is the foyer with reception desk, purser's office, main staircase and lifts. It should be centrally placed in order to receive the passengers so that their immediate needs can be dealt with as soon as they embark. The following public rooms are quite common on most vessels: restaurants, ballroom,

lashing screws to prevent the cargo being lost at sea.

LASH vessels

A lighter is a small barge which may be loaded with cargo. A LASH vessel is a mother ship which is capable of picking up loaded lighters at her stern and stowing them into large holds. (LASH stands for lighter aboard ship). The principle of the system is to collect together several loaded lighters into a rendezvous area with the LASH vessel ready for transportation over seas.

The LASH vessel has a single-strength deck, forward accommodation and a semi-aft engine room. The funnel uptakes are at the sides of the vessel to allow the massive gantry crane to pass down the deck on rails. Longitudinal bulkheads, steel divisions along the length of the vessel, and transverse bulkheads, steel divisions across the vessel, form holds within the ship to stow the lighters in cells. Vertical barge-guides are provided in the holds and the double bottom is equipped with sockets to receive the barge corner posts.

Walkways are provided with interconnecting ladders in the holds for the inspection and maintenance of the lighters. The gantry crane is supported at the stern by two large cantilevers; its lifting capacity is in excess of 500 tons and it is capable of transporting the barge

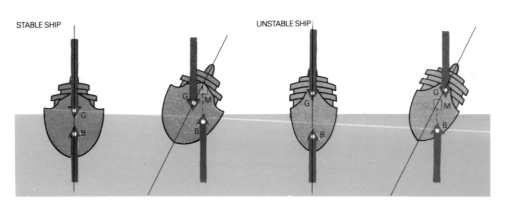

STABLE SHIP

UNSTABLE SHIP

Left: the relative position of the centres of gravity and buoyancy determine a ship's stability. When a ship heels over, the line of action of the buoyancy meets the centreline at a point called the metacentre, M. The ship is unstable if M is below G.

CENTRES OF BOUYANCY AND GRAVITY

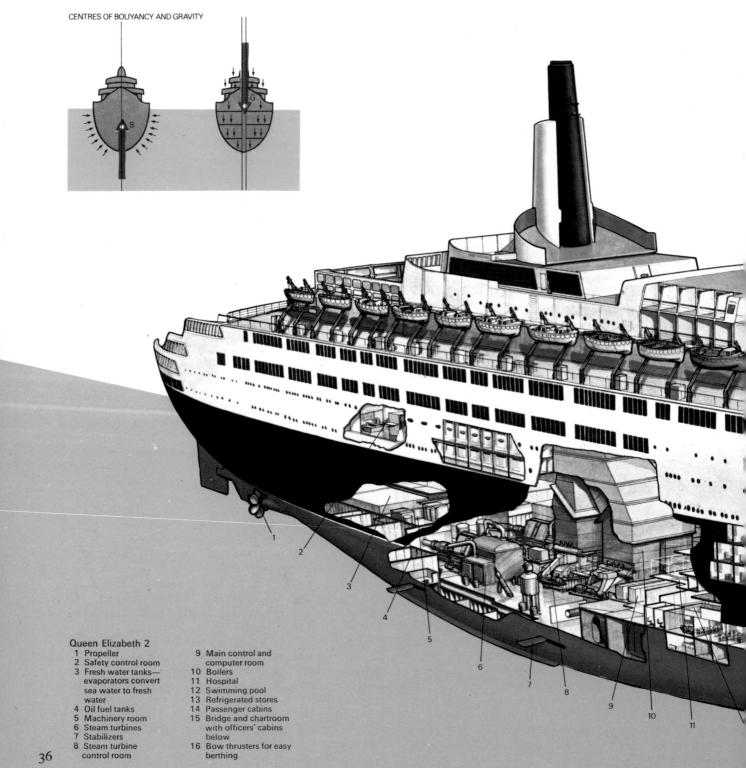

Queen Elizabeth 2
1 Propeller
2 Safety control room
3 Fresh water tanks—
   evaporators convert
   sea water to fresh
   water
4 Oil fuel tanks
5 Machinery room
6 Steam turbines
7 Stabilizers
8 Steam turbine
   control room

9 Main control and
   computer room
10 Boilers
11 Hospital
12 Swimming pool
13 Refrigerated stores
14 Passenger cabins
15 Bridge and chartroom
   with officers' cabins
   below
16 Bow thrusters for easy
   berthing

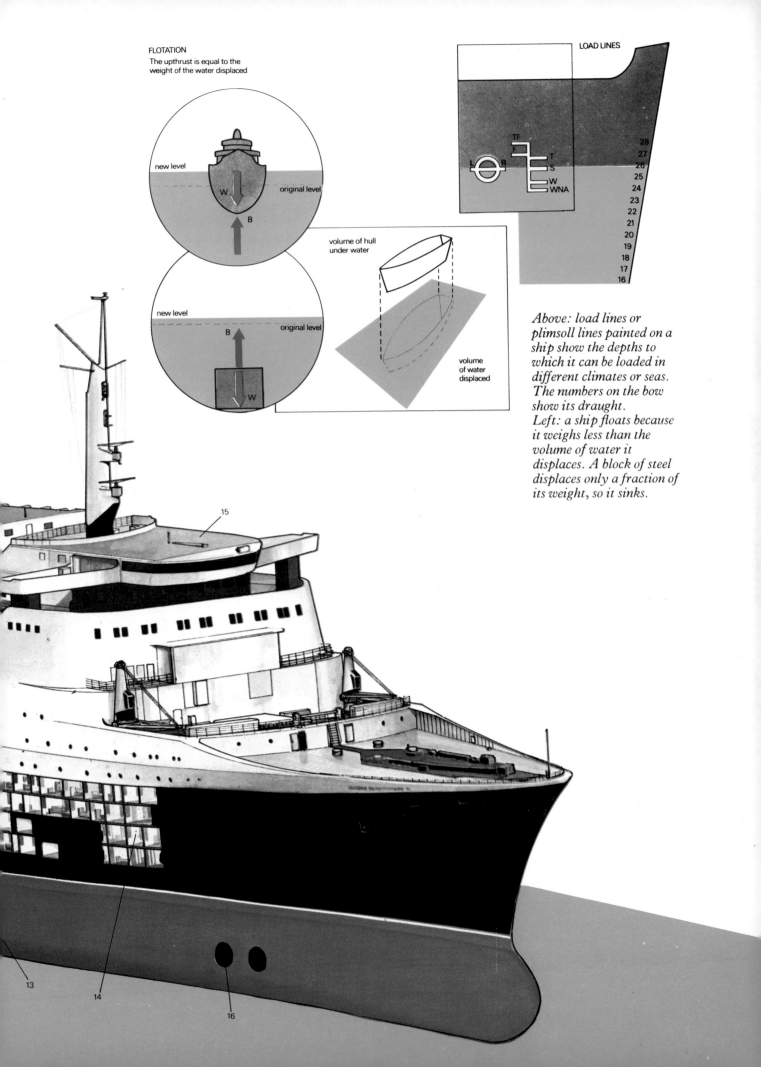

FLOTATION
The upthrust is equal to the
weight of the water displaced

new level

original level

W

B

new level

original level

B

W

volume of hull
under water

volume
of water
displaced

LOAD LINES

TF
F
L R   T
        S
        W
        WNA

28
27
26
25
24
23
22
21
20
19
18
17
16

*Above: load lines or
plimsoll lines painted on a
ship show the depths to
which it can be loaded in
different climates or seas.
The numbers on the bow
show its draught.
Left: a ship floats because
it weighs less than the
volume of water it
displaces. A block of steel
displaces only a fraction of
its weight, so it sinks.*

15

13

14

16

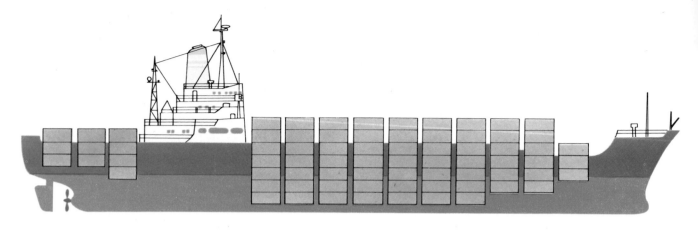

Above: a container ship docked at Manchester. Two of the ship-shore container cranes can be seen. Turnaround time for the ship is minimal.
Next page: a free-path Goliath crane loading a container on to a waiting trailer. The contents of the container will arrive untouched since loading.

cinema, discotheque, shops, cocktail bars, clubrooms, banks and hairdressers. For recreation there will be a swimming pool and a deck area for games, the young children will have a nursery and there are playrooms for older children. The officers are berthed near to the bridge and the remaining crew and stewards have accommodation on a lower deck.

Oil tankers

These vessels have a single main deck and a double bottom in the engine room only. Since tankers are divided into separate compartments, they are considered to be safe enough without having a double bottom along the full length of the ship. To reduce the risk of an explosion, the engines are fitted aft so that the shaft tunnel does not have to pass through any of the oil cargo tanks. At the extreme ends of the cargo tank range there is a cofferdam or bunker space to isolate the cargo from the other parts of the ship. Cofferdams are dry spaces across the vessel, preventing the possibility of any oil leaking directly into an adjacent compartment.

Pumps for discharging the cargo are fitted in a pump room in the bottom of the vessel. This pump room is often part of the cofferdam. The cargo pumps are usually driven by extended spindles from machinery in the main engine room. The oil is discharged from a tank by drawing it into the suctions at the end of a pipe leading from the main cargo pumps. It is then pumped vertically up from the pump room to the main deck where it passes along the deck pipelines until it reaches the deck crossover pipes. These crossovers are connected to the shore installations by hoses which are handled by the shore derrick. Oil tankers have small oiltight hatches with hinged lids giving access to the tanks by long steel ladders which reach to the bottom of the ship. The hatch coaming has a pipe leading vertically upwards to vent off vapour to the atmosphere if there should be a build-up of gas in the tank.

The oil tanks are subdivided by two longitudinal bulkheads into a centre-tank and wing-tanks, port and starboard. Sub-division of the oil tanks controls the movement of the cargo and prevents a large free surface across the ship which would allow the formation of waves in the tank generated by the motion of the ship. This wave will pass up and down the tank and could cause instability or structural damage unless controlled by wash bulkheads.

The engine power of a supertanker is very large, and a single propeller requires six blades so that the thrust is transmitted without overstressing the metal in any part of the blading. A bulbous bow is usually a standard part of the hull for a large tanker and it has the effect of modifying the flow of water at the bow, thereby reducing the power requirements from the ship's engines.

LPG vessels

Vessels of this type are designed to carry propane, butane, anhydrous ammonia and other liquefied gases in specially designed tanks. (LPG stands for liquefied petroleum gas). A typical gas tanker has a design similar to a bulk carrier but it has gas tanks built into the hull which rest on chocks and are keyed to prevent movement when the vessel is rolling or pitching. The

liquid gas temperature in the tanks may be well below zero; this will cause severe thermal stressing when the liquid moves and therefore the tanks will alter in shape owing to temperature changes. A void space between the gas tanks and the hull is filled with an inert gas to prevent the oxygen in the air and any leak of gas from the tank producing an explosive mixture. An inert gas unit in the engine-room is used to produce sufficient gas for the void space and to keep it topped up in case of leakage. The tanks are made from a low-temperature carbon steel which must withstand impact at low temperatures and thus not be susceptible to brittle fracture. In some vessels the gas tanks are not refrigerated but are insulated with four inches (10.1 cm) of polyurethane foam. When the liquid gas vaporizes it collects in domes at the top of the tank where it is drawn off and passed through a reliquefaction plant and then returned to the tank via condensers in liquid form. The domes at the top of each tank project three feet (0.91 m) through the main deck.

Above: the LASH (lighter aboard ship) system. The lighter is a floating container which is towed by a barge to the stern of the ship, where a travelling gantry crane lifts it aboard.

Alternatively there may be no tank refrigeration or reliquefaction plant on the ship and the gas is free to 'boil-off'. The vapour is then transferred to the engine room and used as fuel for the main propulsion. This system makes the vessel less complex, cheaper on plant installation and bunkers but a percentage of the cargo is used over the voyage. Liquid-gas cargo is pumped from the bottom of the tanks using submerged pumps controlled from a room amidships. During pumping, a back pressure must always be maintained to prevent the gas boiling in the pump impeller and creating vapour in the riser when the tank is nearly emptied.

Air in the tanks is displaced before loading the liquid petroleum gas by using the inert gas system. Once the tanks are loaded they will always contain gas, so that the inerting procedure is not employed every time. Gas freeing of a cargo tank can be done by introducing inert-gas until the petroleum is diluted below the flammable limit and then blowing air into the tank and venting the gases at the top of the mast.

Oil Tanker

1	Mooring winches	13	Cargo tank
2	Boiler	14	Mooring winches
3	Crew mess and cabins	15	Access for tank cleaning machinery
4	Radar		
5	Engine rooms	16	Tank hatches
6	Water inlet pipes	17	Steam pipes for cleaning tanks
7	Wheel house, chartroom and radio room		
8	Oil fuel bunker	18	Derricks for lifting pipes on board
9	Ballast tank	19	Discharge and loading points
10	Pump room		
11	Fire tower	20	Anchor winches
12	Fire hydrant	21	Mooring winches

LONGITUDINAL BENDING

WARSHIPS

Up to World War II, the world's navies had fought in conventional naval battles conducted at relatively close quarters with heavy guns. This had led to the favouring of large warships such as the battleship and the slightly smaller cruiser. These had a displacement of over 60,000 tons, carried vast 12 to 18 inch guns, and had an enormous thickness of armour plating—for example, the huge Japanese Yamato of World War II had 25 inch (63.5 cm) armour plating in parts of the turrets and superstructure. It became apparent during World War II that the nature of naval warfare had changed, with less emphasis given to sheer seaborne hitting power and much more to air power. A few torpedoes dropped from small, comparatively cheap aircraft could sink the largest and most expensive battleship. Aircraft range, performance and armament were increasing fast, and so was the technology of the aircraft carrier. Many of the 'naval' battles of the Pacific campaign were fought entirely by aircraft, without warships of either side coming anywhere near each other.

As a result, modern navies have scrapped nearly all their large warships except for aircraft carriers, which must be of a fair size simply in order to have enough space on the flight deck for take-off, landing and parking of aircraft, and below deck for storage, fuel and spares. The US Navy continues to build enormous nuclear-powered carriers. The British Royal Navy, with far less money at its disposal, only has one carrier in commission, but this is less of a disadvantage than it might seem, since it is also being equipped with the vertical take-off 'Harrier' aircraft which can land on a platform on a small, conventional warship.

A typical modern navy consists, apart from aircraft carriers, of frigates, guided missile destroyers, assault ships, patrol boats (or corvettes), minesweepers and submarines.

Frigates

These are small vessels with lengths of just over 300ft (100 m); the 'Leander' class has the largest displacement of 2,200 tons. Since 1945 the frigate has been

developed gradually; the major developments have been in propulsion and armament.

Originally three basic types of frigate were envisaged, each with a primary role: anti-submarine (A/S), anti-aircraft (A/A) and aircraft direction (A/D). Obviously several frigates may be required at one time to cover all of these duties. Eventually a general purpose frigate was designed with the facility for A/S, A/A, and A/D in one hull. It was not equal in performance in any of these roles to frigates that specialized in only one role, but had the advantage of greater flexibility. It was originally intended as an escort for important work or as support for amphibious operations.

Other types, such as the British Type 12 and 'Leander' class, were to be used as fleet escorts, owing to their higher speed and weapon capability. 'Leander' class frigates carry a triple-barrelled anti-submarine mortar and a 'Wasp' helicopter armed with anti-submarine torpedoes. Some 'Leanders' are fitted with a quadruple 'Seacat' missile launcher and two 4.5 in guns, others are armed with a further improved anti-submarine weapon, 'Ikara'. An improved sonar installation including an over-the-stern variable-depth sonar is now fitted, and the vessels have a non-retractable fin type stabilizer.

As costs in shipbuilding have risen, new vessels have had a price limitation imposed. A recent British frigate type built to this limit, the Type 21, has a length of 384 ft (117.1 m) and a displacement of 2,500 tons. Propulsion consists of two Olympus gas turbines for high power and two Tyne gas turbines for economical cruising. A power of 37 MW gives the Type 21 a speed of 34 knots. Armament consists of one single 4.5 in gun, two 20 mm anti-aircraft guns, one quadruple 'Seacat' missile, torpedo tubes and one helicopter.

The Bismarck was destroyed in a deadly hide-and-seek game by the Royal Navy during World War II. Such battleships are obsolete now because they are too easy to destroy with modern weapons.

'River' class frigate.

Construction

Heavy plating is not fitted to any modern warships. The side plating thickness of a frigate is less than that of many of the larger merchant vessels. Armour plating will not resist modern weapons, and it increases the displacement so that more power is required to propel the vessel at speed.

The hull is prefabricated and of all-welded construction with T-bars used for stiffening in the longitudinal direction. A grillage hull structure is the best design to resist underwater explosions and shock. It is formed by passing the T-bar longitudinally through the larger transverse framing, forming squares of stiffening to support the shell plates. The grillage structure gives the most efficient form of stiffening for minimum weight. Special quality steel is used in regions of the hull where there are high stresses, to reduce the possibility of cracks. To prevent corrosion, the steel is shot-blasted to remove mill scale and rust, and is then painted. Some parts of the vessel particularly susceptible to corrosion are shot blasted and zinc sprayed after construction. Weight can be saved by using aluminium for the superstructures, but it must be restricted to areas not likely to be subjected to blast, as it has a low melting point. Abrupt changes in the shape of superstructures, such as the forecastle and the long midship superstructure, cause a loss in strength; for this reason gradual changes are made by sloping the ends of these structures.

Watertight subdivision is essential to keep the ship afloat in the event of damage; this is achieved by fitting a number of watertight transverse bulkheads, longitudinal bulkheads, decks and watertight flats. The transverse bulkheads are usually stiffened vertically and the plates comprising the bulkhead are welded together horizontally. The T-bar longitudinals are connected strongly to the bulkheads with stiffeners to help integrate the structure. Access through the bulkhead is often necessary and therefore watertight doors are fitted, but they must be above the deep waterline level and all watertight compartments not normally occupied are closed when the vessel is at sea.

Lattice masts were common on many Royal Navy vessels, but the weight of the modern equipment, such as the large radar scanner, has led to the introduction of the plate mast, which is stronger and less prone to vibration. The inside of the mast protects the cables and junction boxes which connect the aerials and radar.

A modern frigate is capable of running in a closed down condition in case of a nuclear attack; this means that special precautions are necessary to prevent contamination through the ventilation systems. In the upper structure, radar room, communications control room, computer rooms, electronic warfare office and an enclosed bridge are now common. The No. 1 deck accommodation consists of the wardroom, officers' and petty officers' berths, galley, recreation rooms and sick bay. No. 2 deck is subdivided into gunbays, power rooms, gunners' stores, weapons spare gear store, the senior and junior ratings dining hall, galley, scullery, 'Seacat' magazine, ship control centre, engineers' workshop and accommodation for junior ratings. The No. 3 deck contains the sonar instrument room, junior ratings' mess, refrigeration stores and fuel stores. Finally, in the bottom of the vessel, are the magazine and diesel oil tanks; there is also provision for the helicopter fuel, lubricating oil and the sonar space.

Guided missile destroyers

The guided missile destroyer (GMD) is larger than a frigate, and often approaches the size of the older conventional cruiser. The Royal Navy 'County' class, for example, displaces 6,309 tons. The armament consists of four 4.5 inch guns, a beam riding (radar controlled) 'Seaslug' ship-to-air missile, two 'Seacat' missiles, and a 'Wessex' helicopter with homing torpedoes to act as an anti-submarine weapon. The crew of 36 officers and 459 ratings have fully air conditioned living and working spaces. A powered lift is used to connect the bridge with the operations room and action information centre which are installed on a lower deck.

Right: a guided missile cruiser of the Soviet Navy, now possibly the most powerful navy in the world.
Opposite page: the upper superstructure of the frigate HMS Charybdis, showing radar scanners, a typical plate mast and a multiple Seacat missile launcher.
The art work shows a type 82 guided missile destroyer. The HMS Bristol displaces 6000 tons.

Cruiser 'Long Beach'.

HMS BRISTOL
1 Laundry
2 Anti-submarine mortar
3 Helicopter flight deck
4 Sea Dart missiles
5 Mess decks
6 Missile control radar
7 Funnels for gas turbines
8 Surface search radar
9 Engine rooms
10 Funnel for steam turbines
11 Air search radar
12 Ikara control radar
13 Ikara missiles
14 4.5 in gun

Exposed decks are designed simply, to allow washing down in the event of contamination by nuclear fallout.

In later vessels, apart from improvements to the 'Seacat' missile and sonar, an integrated communications system, action data automation, tactical information data evaluation and a ship's inertial navigational system are fitted.

A Type 82 GMD, built on the Tyne and launched in 1969, can operate under closed down conditions in case of fallout, and it has a greater weapon potential than earlier vessels of this size. The vessel is a general purpose type designed to defend surface forces against air and surface attack. It can hunt and destroy submarines, and can act as a radar picket and direct aircraft. As an independent unit the vessel can carry out police duties in any part of the world.

The very latest Type 42 GMD was designed for a price, just as the Type 21 frigate. This vessel has design standards similar to the improved 'Leander' class frigate, except in the case of the main propulsion machinery. Contrary to normal Royal Naval practice this vessel is not given extra spaces for future modifications and there is a restiction on weight.

Some items have been pruned to save money, for example only one anchor and cable gear is fitted, but some equipment such as stabilizers to assist the guided weapon system are retained. The two Olympus and two Tyne gas turbines give a similar output to that of the Type 21 frigate, but the speed is slightly reduced as the Type 42 is a larger vessel with a displacement of 3718 tons.

The steering gear chosen for this vessel is of the rotary vane type, which is an innovation for warships, although merchant vessels have used this type of steering gear for a number of years.

Armament for the vessel makes it suitable for worldwide operation and consists of a 'Seadart' missile system served by two tracker illumination radars,

Above top: the frigate Dat Assawari, *of the Libyan Navy, built in Britain.*
Above: a Boeing Sea Knight anti-submarine helicopter and a light assault ship arrive home at the same time.

Above: the nuclear-powered USS Enterprise. *Below:* HMS Buttercup, *a minesweeper, was built in 1941-42 in Belfast.*

target indication and long range warning facilities, together with a Mk 8 4.5 in gun with a high automatic rate of fire and a 'Lynx' torpedo carrying helicopter.

Assault ships

The vessel is used to transport and land heavy military equipment and men when there are no port facilities. The vessel carries two types of landing craft, one for personnel and light equipment and the other for tanks and other heavy vehicles. An assault ship can carry four of the large landing craft in a floodable dock compartment at the end. Troops are transferred to their landing craft from No. 1 deck when the craft is lowered from the davits and *bowsed* into (held against) the ship's side to prevent relative motion. Inside the dock there are *batter boards* to prevent damage to the landing craft or the ship and there is a sloping apron up to the tank deck level to act as a beach to reduce the wave motion in the dock, and as a *hard* (loading area) for the landing craft. This apron is built up of steel gratings. A hinged gate is used at the after end to close the dock.

The dock floor is above the waterline and the space is dry during transit, but for a seaborne assault the ballast tanks in the vessel are quickly flooded to bring the ship down to a deep draught and so flood the dock. Vehicle spaces are well protected by steel bulkheads and the ventilation system is designed to remove fuel vapour and dangerous gases.

The vessel is heavily stiffened to withstand the variations in loading due to ballasting and cargo movements. No. 1 deck, over the dock, must withstand the dynamic weight of the helicopter and requires heavy deck beams for support, as pillars can not be used in this region. The tank deck is supported by rows of pillars fitted in the vehicle space below, which are in turn supported by the bottom structure in the ship; water ballast tanks are arranged over the length of the bottom structure, with fuel tanks and stores in the centre portion.

Steam turbines are used for main propulsion and the engine room is below the vehicle deck. Accommodation is fitted forward and in the superstructure, and various stores are arranged on lower decks.

Orthodox landing craft may be replaced at a future date by hovercraft which could reduce the run-in time to establish a beachhead.

Aircraft carriers

Aircraft carriers are complex ships with very special requirements. Their decks must be well above the waterline so that aircraft can land in bad weather, and must also be clear, with the bridge and funnel on the starboard side forming an 'island'. The hangar deck must be a clear space with a depth extending through two decks. To avoid passing the boiler uptakes through the hangar deck, they are led across to the starboard side and then up to the funnel.

Armanent to protect the 43,000 ton British 'Ark Royal' consists of several quadruple 'Seacat' missile launchers situated on sponsons around the sides of the ship, over thirty aircraft and about six helicopters. The flight deck must be long enough to give sufficient landing area aft and catapult length forward to accelerate the heaviest aircraft. Angled flight decks are required to give the necessary deck length to land aircraft in rapid succession. Once the aircraft has

been arrested, it is moved to the starboard forward corner of the flight deck to give a clear space to allow any aircraft that has missed the arresting wires to fly off the end of the angled deck and to return for another landing attempt.

Two aircraft lifts serving both ends of the hangar for transportation to and from the flight deck are operated electrically, using a chain driven system. To maintain the aircraft, several workshops are arranged around the hangar on the port and starboard sides of the ship. Aircraft munitions and aircraft fuel are stored in lower regions of the vessel to give maximum protection. A long-range radar, radio communication and computers are necessary for tracking high-speed aircraft, and space must be provided for this equipment along with briefing, aircraft control, hangar control and flying control position rooms.

At the after end of the catapult, protection from the jet blast is necessary to prevent following aircraft from being damaged by hot exhaust gases. The deck panels must also be water cooled in this region to avoid overheating.

Firefighting arrangements on these vessels are extremely important and the hangars can be quickly drenched by a sprinkler system operated from remotely controlled pumps.

Catapult

When aircraft carriers first appeared in the 1920s the aircraft were so light and slow that they could take off from the relatively small deck space available under their own power. But as they became heavier, the amount of deck used for take off became prohibitive, and catapults were therefore introduced at the forward end of the ship to accelerate them up to flying speed within an acceptably short distance.

The standard type of catapult used for three decades employed hydro-pneumatic actuation to generate the launch energy required. Compressed air stored in large bottles below the deck was the propulsive agent used to drive a piston along a cylinder. The motion of the piston was transmitted to the aircraft through a system of cables and pulleys, and the equipment was reset after launch by means of hydraulic pressure applied to the piston in the reverse direction.

By the end of World War II it had become evident that any development of the hydro-pneumatic catapult, needed to launch the substantially heavier turbine-powered aircraft then in prospect, would be impracticable. The size and complexity of the air pumping system, and the increasing weight of the cable needed—up to $7\frac{1}{2}$ tons, all of which had to be accelerated to take off speed and then decelerated again—were rapidly becoming unacceptable owing to the space and power required to provide adequate performance. The breakthrough came with the slotted-cylinder technique proposed by Cdr C C Mitchell.

This idea dispensed with the complexity of cables and pulleys by connecting the piston directly to the aircraft by means of a lever protruding through the side of the cylinder. Since the piston travels the length of the cylinder, a slot has to be cut along the piston to accommodate the driving arm, and this immediately leads to the problem of how to seal the cylinder against pressure loss without interrupting the movement of the piston. This was solved by the development of a sealing strip, arranged so that it could be moved from its seat as the piston passed by, and then pressed back into place.

At the same time, a re-appraisal was made of the propulsive technology available and several methods, including the use of the explosive cordite, were studied. These investigations showed the superiority of steam power to the other alternatives, and steam was readily available from the ship's turbine propulsion system.

The steam catapult was first used experimentally aboard the light fleet carrier *HMS Perseus* in 1949. In 1953 it was adapted by the Royal Navy as the standard replacement for the older type, and was shortly afterwards chosen by the United States Navy.

Installations vary from ship to ship, but the one

Opposite page: a Phantom F4B is about to be catapulted from the USS Forrestal. *The plane carries a Sparrow and two Sidewinder missiles.*

installed on *HMS Ark Royal* is typical. Two catapults, each about 200 ft (61 m) long, can apply more than 4 'g' acceleration ('g' is a measurement of acceleration equivalent to that of the Earth's gravity and is 32 ft/sec² or 9.81 m/sec²) to the heaviest aircraft operated from the ship.

Each catapult consists of two piston and cylinder combinations lying alongside one another in the fore-and-aft direction of the deck. The pistons are connected to a common shuttle by means of keyed joints. On the shuttle is a towing block which protrudes through the deck, transmitting the motion of the pistons to the aircraft by means of a bridle. The moving assembly within each cylinder actually consists of a double piston on a common shaft, with the driving flange mounted between them. This enables the sealing strip in the cylinder to remain in place until the driving piston has passed by, preventing both loss of steam pressure and distortion of the cylinder (which would permit leaks past the piston) under the influence of this pressure. The cylinder is several feet in diameter, while the sealing strip has a cross-section of about $1\frac{1}{8}$ inch by $\frac{7}{16}$ inch (28mm × 11 mm).

At the end of their travel the shuttle and pistons are brought to rest by means of a retardation cylinder in the bows of the ship. Because it lies on its side and not vertically, this damping cylinder has to kept full of water by means of a spray system which directs a jet of fluid spirally around its inside walls. After launch, the shuttle and pistons are reset by means of a hydraulically operated jigger which causes a grab to pull the shuttle back to the starting position.

The steam system employs large bottles supplied by the ship's boilers, with valves to admit steam to the catapult cylinders at the moment of launch. The launch speed is varied, according to the needs of the aircraft, by adjusting the steam pressure.

Arresting mechanism

When an aircraft lands on an aircraft carrier deck, its speed has to be cut from perhaps 150 mile/h (240 km/h) to rest in about 200 ft (60 m). The aircraft may well weigh up to 50,000 lb (23 tonnes), so the kinetic energy—the energy of motion—to be dissipated is considerable.

At the same time the retardation must be smooth: there must be no sudden snatch which might break the pilot's neck, overstress the aircraft's frame or disturb its landing path. Ideally, the retardation should be progressive, starting from nothing, building up to a maximum, then remaining constant until the aircraft finally comes to a standstill.

Arresting mechanisms are designed to achieve this aim, and in principle they all operate in the same way. At its tail end, the aircraft is fitted with a hinged hook which hangs below the level of the wheels of the aircraft during the landing run. As the plane comes in over the deck the hook engages with a steel arresting wire stretched across the deck and raised a few inches

Above: one of nine Turkish 'Kartal' class torpedo boats launching a Penguin missile.
Opposite page: the hydrofoil USS Pegasus with a Harpoon missile launcher. Top inset: the Israeli Gabriel missile: below, the Italian Otomat.

by bow-shaped steel springs to allow the hook underneath. The ends of the arresting wire are connected to the energy absorbing gear, which has been further developed over the last few years to cater for the increasing weight of modern aircraft.

The absorbing system widely used on British and American craft is based on the ram effect of a piston pushing hydraulic fluid through a control or throttling valve. As the arresting wire is pulled out it runs through guiding pulley wheels—or, in naval terms, sheaves—which transfer the movement to the ram through a series of pulleys mounted on both the fixed cylinder and the moving ram housed below deck.

Movement of the main arresting wire by, say, a distance of 16 ft moves the final pulley, which is coupled to the piston, by only 1 ft. This reduction in movement keeps the size of the piston within bounds and gives a useful mechanical advantage.

The retarding force is actually the hydraulic pressure in the cylinder, which depends on the ram speed. As the aircraft and therefore the ram slows, this force would decrease. So that the retardation remains constant, the control valve is arranged to provide greater restriction as more wire is pulled out. This can be adjusted to allow for different weights.

The outflow from the hydraulic cylinder goes into a chamber, where it compresses a gas to store the energy. This energy is used to reset the system and pull the arresting wire back to its original position, the compressed gas forcing the hydraulic fluid back into the cylinder with the aid of a pump to overcome the energy losses in the system.

Resetting at speed is important when a large number of aircraft have to be landed in a short time. After an aircraft has landed, the arresting wire is inspected quickly for faults and then is pulled back tight across the deck, the operation taking about 20 seconds.

The high weights of modern aircraft have made this arrangement unsuitable where deck space is limited. American vessels are larger than British built craft, and they have extended the flight deck to take the longer stopping space required. But in 1968, Britain's

Ark Royal aircraft carrier was converted to a different system. The arresting wire remains but, instead of a hydraulic ram, a low-energy water spray system is used.

By contrast to the older system of pulleys, the new water spray is direct acting. A sheave takes the wire below decks as before but this time there is no mechanical reduction and the wire acts directly on a piston in a water filled cylinder 200 ft (60 m) long. Along this cylinder is a series of holes which are closed off progressively as the arresting wire is extended, giving a nearly constant force. Water sprays out of the holes but is caught by an outer cylinder around the main one.

An advantage of this system is that it can be programmed to cater for a whole range of aircraft weighing from 10,000 to 50,000 lb (4.5 to 23 tonnes). It has, however, created a number of design problems—now overcome. Resetting time must still be as quick as the earlier system and this means moving the piston back over its entire length in perhaps 20 seconds, while making sure that the cylinder is completely full of water: any air pockets could give disastrous shocks to the aircraft being slowed down. One method of resetting uses a return arrangement based on a hydraulic cylinder and a series of pulleys.

Patrol boats

These are used by many nations for police work along their coasts, and for rescue operations. Some vessels have anti-submarine weapons and are well armed with guns. The majority are very fast and some, belonging to the US Navy, are fitted with hydrofoils. Many are powered by gas turbines. A conventional gunboat will have accommodation for officers, senior and junior ratings. The gun is armed from a revolving magazine below deck at the forward end. The operations room, enclosed bridge and radio room are situated on the strength deck just aft of the gun. Twin diesels

51

SUBMARINES

power the boat, and the engine room contains two alternators and a control room with the main switchboard. Some nations have vessels which are between the size of a frigate and a patrol boat. These vessels are called *corvettes*, and they can perform most of the peacetime duties of a frigate with greater economy, while providing training for naval personnel.

Minesweepers

Minesweepers are small vessels, the largest coastal type being 153 feet (46.6 m) length and 360 tons displacement, the smaller type—inshore minesweepers—are 100 feet (30.5 m) in length and have a displacement of 120 tons. Their main function is to clear shipping lanes into port by sweeping and recovering mines. Equipment on board the vessel must be capable of dealing with the several types of mine.

Buoyant mines connected with a wire to a sinker are moored to the seabed and will explode on contact with a ship's hull. The minesweeper's paravane will cut the wire holding the mine, which can then be destroyed by gunfire when it floats to the surface.

The paravane is a kind of underwater kite and it consists of a torpedo-like body having *planes*, looking rather like aircraft wings, projecting on each side. It is buoyant, and depends on a downward force on the planes when it is towed along to keep it underwater. An elevator situated at the tail is controlled by a preset hydrostatic device within the body and automatically keeps the paravane at the correct predetermined depth. The paravane is towed, or *streamed*, from the forefoot of a ship (directly below the bow), and rides well away from the side at about the same depth as the ship's keel. The mooring wire of a mine which lies in the path of a paravane wire will be snagged and forced to slide away from the ship towards the paravane. The towing wire is so constructed that it saws through the mine mooring wire while it slides along, but if the sawing action fails to cut the mine's wire completely, a cutting device completes the task.

During the minesweeping operations, two paravanes are streamed, one on each side of the ship. They are attached to the ship by means of a V-shaped *towing shoe*, which can be hauled up or down the stem (the front part of the bow). A wire for hauling up the towing shoe runs directly on to the foredeck through the *bullring*, while a downhaul wire leads through a vertical pipe built into the ship's stem. To begin streaming, the towing shoe is hauled right up to deck level in order to shackle on the paravane wires. The shoe is then hauled down to its deep towing position and the paravanes are launched overboard.

Paravanes were used by most classes of warship, including destroyers, cruisers, battleships and aircraft carriers, in both World Wars. They were also used by a few merchant ships whose voyages took them unescorted near or through mined waters. Paravanes are not normally fitted to warships today, but can be quickly added if required.

Although the principle of the diving bell has been known for over 2000 years, and Leonardo da Vinci produced drawings for underwater craft, not until William Bourne, an English naval officer, produced a treatise on the principles of under-water ballasting in 1580, were the practicalities examined. It was then realized that, by applying Archimedes' principle of a floating body displacing a quantity of water equal to its own weight, it was possible to build a craft fitted with ballast tanks into which water could be admitted, thereby increasing its weight sufficiently for the craft to submerge. Conversely, the expulsion of the added water would allow the craft once more to float upon the surface. It was on this basic plan that Cornelius van Drebbel, a Dutch mechanic, built what is believed to have been the first boat which not only went below the surface but also returned at will. His craft, which was demonstrated to King James I in the Thames off Westminster, used an expanding leather bulkhead which could be screwed back into position to expel the ballast water. Propulsion was by means of oars and a breathing tube led to the surface. Drebbel successfully navigated from Westminster to Greenwich.

Early submarines

During the 17th and 18th centuries a number of attempts were made to design more efficient underwater craft—in 1653 the Frenchman de Son produced a submersible propelled by a clockwork-driven paddlewheel, which was not a success. Other schemes were tried for adding the necessary ballast to dive a boat and two Englishmen built practical craft, the first, Symons, using leather bottles which filled with water. In 1773 Day sailed into Plymouth sound in a boat which relied on external ballast in the shape of rocks to destroy its surface buoyancy. These were to be released from within to regain the surface, but Day was the first submarine casualty. With no means of controlling his depth and possibly experiencing difficulty in jettisoning his ballast, it seems likely that his craft was crushed by the water pressure.

Only three years later David Bushnell, an American seeking methods of attacking British ships during the War of Independence, built the *Turtle*. She was a one-man, egg-shaped craft driven by a propeller operated by a crank, and she carried a charge of 150 lb (68 kg) of gun powder with a timing mechanism fitted. In 1776 the first submarine attack on a warship was carried out, being thwarted only by the fact that the screw securing the charge to the flagship's hull struck metal and would not penetrate. In 1800 a large and more ambitious submersible, the *Nautilus*, was built by another American, Robert Fulton. This succeeded in sinking ships in two trial attacks but was never used in action. With only hand propulsion, no means of accurate depth control and with a weapon which required contact with the target, the submersible was not yet suitable for operational use.

It was not until 1850 that any progress was made,

but from this point onwards the development of submersible craft was to advance rapidly. In that year Wilhelm Bauer, a Bavarian, produced a boat with a cast iron hull and the germ of a trimming system in which weights were moved fore and aft. She was equipped with a hand driven screw. In 1863, when the French produced the *Plongeur* with compressed air stored in bottles to operate the engine and blow the ballast tanks, the first major mechanical aids were incorporated in submarine design. In the same year, steam driven craft, the *Davids*, were used in the American Civil War.

From this time various methods of propulsion—heat storage, steam engines, electric motors and petrol [gasoline] engines—were employed but the greatest advances were made by John P. Holland, an Irishman who had emigrated to the USA, and Laubeuf of France. The series of craft designed and built by the former and the handsome *Narval* which the latter completed in 1899 were the true forerunners of today's fleets.

By the early years of the 20th century all the major naval powers were forced into an interest in this new form of warfare, and submarine design followed the general principles which continued to the present day.

Modern design

The strength of the main pressure hull determines the depth to which the boat can dive. Of steel construction, its plates were originally riveted together but this has now been replaced by welding. The usual description of 'cigar-shaped' is approximately accurate—the cross section should be circular to obtain maximum strength and should be pierced by as few holes as possible. These are normally confined to the access hatches, the torpedo tube openings, the sleeves for periscopes and masts, escape hatches (normally secured shut in wartime), the engine-exhaust system and snort-mast (snorkel) leads, some of the trim tanks (see below) and the log (speed indicator). Each is equipped with a method of closure which is tested to full pressure.

Outside the pressure hull are built the conning tower, the casing and the ballast tanks, which are either of the saddle tank type, great bulges hung from the main structure, or of the double hull type in which a whole skin is wrapped about the pressure hull, Some sub-

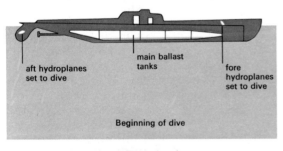

aft hydroplanes
set to dive

main ballast
tanks

fore
hydroplanes
set to dive

Beginning of dive

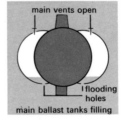

main vents open

flooding
holes

main ballast tanks filling

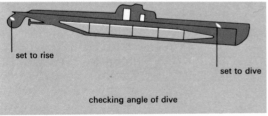

set to rise

set to dive

checking angle of dive

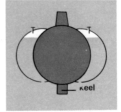

keel

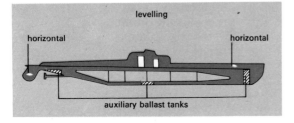

levelling

horizontal

horizontal

auxiliary ballast tanks

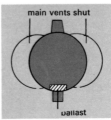

main vents shut

ballast

Left: submarines dive by flooding the main ballast tanks and using the hydroplanes at speed. The angle of dive is controlled by the relative angles of front and rear hydroplanes. At the desired depth the boat is levelled by flooding small internal ballast tanks.

marines, notably the British 'U' and 'V' class, were fitted with internal ballast tanks in which the tanks were fitted within the pressure hull, but this arrangement, requiring additional penetration of the pressure hull, seriously reduced the diving-depth and is no longer employed.

Each ballast tank must have two openings: one at the bottom to let in the water ballast required on diving and through which that water is expelled by compressed air on surfacing, and one on the top through which air may escape to allow the water to enter. The lower opening can be merely a hole at the bottom of the tank, in which case the tank is known as free-flooding, or it may have a valve fitted, known as a Kingston valve. The valve on the top, which retains the air under slight pressure within the tank, is the main vent.

Diving

The act of diving the submarine is achieved by having all Kingston valves open and then opening the main vents, thus releasing the air pressure which has previously kept the tanks dry. This reduces the submarine to the state known as neutral buoyancy, in other words the slightest downward force causes the craft to sink.

This fact, by itself, will not take the submarine below the surface. Without other aids she would wallow in a dangerous state on the surface. She must be driven below the surface, and this is achieved by the thrust of the propellers forcing her forward and the hydroplanes, placed two forward and two aft, directing her downwards.

Once below the surface it is necessary to 'catch a trim'. This means that, having achieved neutral

Above: a nuclear-powered submarine equipped with Polaris missiles is one of the world's deadliest weapons.
Below: the forward torpedo compartment of the nuclear-powered HMS Resolution. Torpedos are still carried by modern submarines in case they have to engage surface ships or other subs.
Below right: the missile compartment of a Polaris submarine. The vessel carries sixteen missiles which can be launched while submerged and have a range of up to 2800 miles (4500 km).

54

buoyancy, she must have the weights within her so adjusted that, at the desired depth, she will remain static and horizontal. This state is achieved by transferring water into and out of trim tanks situated at either end and amidships. The deeper the submarine goes, the greater the compression of her hull and the less becomes her displacement. As a result, more water must be expelled from her trim tanks to ensure that her displacement always equals her weight. Only then will the submarine be in the state known as stopped trim, when she can hover at the desired depth

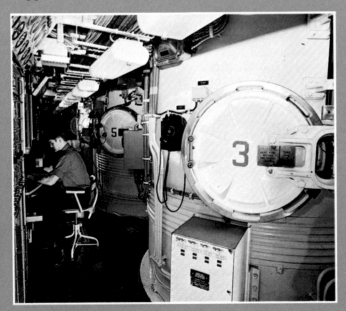

without any mechanical assistance.

Propulsion

The means of propulsion for submarines was not satisfactorily solved until the diesel engine was incorporated in the design. Steam propulsion, though occasionally used in later years, presented the major problems of the necessity for a funnel, the delay in shutting-down the boilers before diving and the subsequent latent heat from those boilers. Petrol [gasoline] engines produced fumes which were occasionally explosive and presented the difficulty of storing a highly volatile fuel. The heavy oil engine, followed by the diesel, overcame most of these problems. It provided a means of propulsion using low flash-point fuel, an instant ability to dive even though the engines were running, and simpler and more dependable machinery. Today, in the normal patrol submarine, diesel engines provide the power required on the surface for propulsion and for charging the batteries. As the majority of such boats are now equipped with snort masts, which take air from the surface at periscope depth (up to 50 ft, 15.2 m), both these functions can now be carried out below the surface. Propulsion on the surface or at periscope depth can be either by direct drive, in which the diesel is coupled through a clutch to the main electric motors and through a tail clutch to the screw, or by diesel-electric drive in which the diesel drives a generator which provides power for the main electric motors to rotate the propellor.

When below periscope depth, propulsion is by means of the main motors, which draw their power from large storage batteries below the main deck. These are

Above: the USS Henry Clay *nuclear submarine running at speed on the surface. She carries sixteen Poseidon nuclear weapons.*

charged, when the diesels are running, either from the generators in a diesel-electric boat or from the main motors acting as generators in a direct-drive boat.

In nuclear submarines a coolant liquid is pumped in a closed circuit between a nuclear reactor, where it takes up heat from the radioactive core, and a boiler heat-exchanger, where it gives up the heat to a water feed, thereby generating steam. The steam is conducted through valves to the main propulsion turbines and auxiliary turbines which generate power for subsidiary systems. The main propulsion turbine can drive the screw, either directly through a speed reduction gear or by means of a turboelectric drive (like diesel-electric drive, but with a steam turbine replacing the diesel engine).

Subsidiary systems are needed for many purposes. Hydraulic power operates the periscopes, the raising and lowering of the snort and other masts, the opening and shutting of the torpedo tube bow caps, the control of the main vents on the ballast tanks and many other minor yet vital items. Few systems these days are hand operated and most are electronically controlled.

Submarine periscopes

In a submarine periscope the top window is sometimes 50 ft (15 m) above the eye lens and the tube only up to 10 in (25 cm) in diameter, so a number of telescope lens systems are fitted to maintain the field of view. Two types of periscopes are fitted in submarines, a monocular type with a small diameter top tube, and a binocular type with a larger top tube for light gathering. Binocular vision is achieved by fitting two aligned

optical systems into the same tube. Because of an optical illusion, objects seen through a tube look smaller than they really are, and it is therefore necessary to introduce some magnification into a periscope system. The normal lens system gives a magnification of six, but a $\frac{1}{4}$ times diminishing telescope can be introduced to give an overall magnification of $1\frac{1}{2}$. This gives the observer a more accurate impression of object size.

Light enters the periscope through a top window. It is reflected by a prism which directs the rays down the periscope tube, through the diminishing telescope (if inserted), and through an *objective lens* which brings the rays to a *focal point*, where a *graticule* is fitted. The graticule is usually a cross etched into a lens to act as a sighting mark. The light then passes through another objective lens. To minimize vibration of the image in the eye lens when the submarine is moving, another telescope system is fitted which directs the image formed at the graticule to a point where vibration has the least effect. The light then passes in parallel rays between the two main tube lenses. The bottom main tube lens focuses the rays through a prism, which reflects the rays into the horizontal, and on to a *field lens* where the image is observed through an *eye lens* which can be focused to suit the individual. In binocular periscopes a second pair of prisms is fitted in the eyepiece, enabling the distance between the eye lenses to be adjusted. It is possible to introduce another prism into the system for mounting a camera.

The top prism can be pivoted vertically to scan above and below the horizon by means of a rack and pinion mechanism operated through pulleys and wires from the *left training handle* at the bottom of the periscope. The diminishing, or change power telescope

Left: the USS Sam Rayburn, shown with all sixteen of her missile hatches open.

can be inserted or removed from the lens system in the same way, but the control is located on the *right training handle*.

A pair of contra-rotating prisms, called the *estimator*, can be inserted above the bottom prism by means of a handle and gearing. When rotated, these prisms produce a ghost image. If the base of the ghost image is placed at the top of the real image, the angle subtended by this movement can be read on a scale, and if the height of the object is known, its range can be calculated. The periscope is usually equipped with a small calculator for this purpose.

In some periscopes a sextant is fitted, the light for this system entering through a window below the top main window. Normally, a horizon has to be visible for sextant readings to be taken, but in some cases it is possible to take sightings when no horizon is visible by introducing an artificial horizon. This is achieved by building into the periscope a complex system of lenses, calculators and a gyro to keep the equipment stable in the horizontal plane, regardless of the relative motion of the boat.

The periscope is supported by a bracket, called a *crosshead*, which is attached to twin hydraulic hoists which move the periscope up or down through a gland and bearings so that it protrudes out of the submarine fin. In the crosshead are devices which transmit the bearings of objects to various computers in the submarine. The modern periscope is not purely for observation, it is an integral part of a submarine's weapons and navigation systems.

Navigation

In the early days navigation of submarines was rightly described as 'by guess and by God'. The early submarines had no periscopes and, when these were introduced, some projected an inverted picture on a ground glass screen. Later improvements provided increased ability to examine the sky as well as the sea; these include radar ranging and low light television scanning in addition to periscope sextants for taking Sun and star sightings. Today, the need for a point of land for a periscope fix, or the tedious business of surfacing to allow the navigator to take a sun, moon or star sighting, is gone. SINS (Submarine Inertial Navigation System), a complex of gyroscopes, now produces a remarkably accurate plot which requires 'up-dating' from external fixes only every few days. Assisted by the well-tried navigation aids of radar and echo sounding, the submarine navigator is today as well placed to know his exact position as anyone.

Armament

The submarine's weaponry has improved beyond recognition over the years. The original screwed charge was replaced by the spar torpedo (an explosive charge secured to the end of a long spar). Whitehead perfected his mobile torpedo in the 1870s, and this soon became the natural equipment for underwater craft. Originally dropped from collars on the upper deck, they were soon ejected from tubes projecting from the pressure hull which, provided the submarine was fitted with efficient bow caps, allowed reloading to take place. Methods of aiming these torpedoes progressed from 'eye shooting' to the modern computer controlled system. The gun was for many years a valuable weapon, but it was eventually defeated by the ability of radar to detect a submarine the moment it surfaced. Now the gun's function of striking from above the sea has been taken over by the cruise missile and the submarine has an overall armoury outranging and outperforming any surface ship except in the sphere of aircraft defence. With the possibility of fitting nuclear warheads to any of their weapons, various classes of submarines in the major fleets now carry ballistic missiles such as *Polaris* (range about 2800 miles, 4500 km) and its successor *Poseidon* (range about 3000 miles, 4800 km) for long range strikes, cruise missiles covering 250 miles (400 km) to short range, and torpedoes equipped with passive or active homing heads as well as wire guidance for close range. Information to programme and control this wide armoury of weapons comes from shore control, aircraft reconnaissance, the submarine's own radar and sonar, as well as the well-tried sighting through the periscope.

The whole aspect of submarine operations was changed when the *USS Nautilus* got underway on nuclear power in January 1955. From then on it was possible for a true submarine, as opposed to her submersible predecessors who were dependent on the atmosphere for their support, to operate for years without refuelling, to manufacture her own air and fresh water, to travel at sustained speeds hitherto unknown in the submarine world, and to remain totally submerged for periods impossible for diesel boats.

THE HYDROFOIL

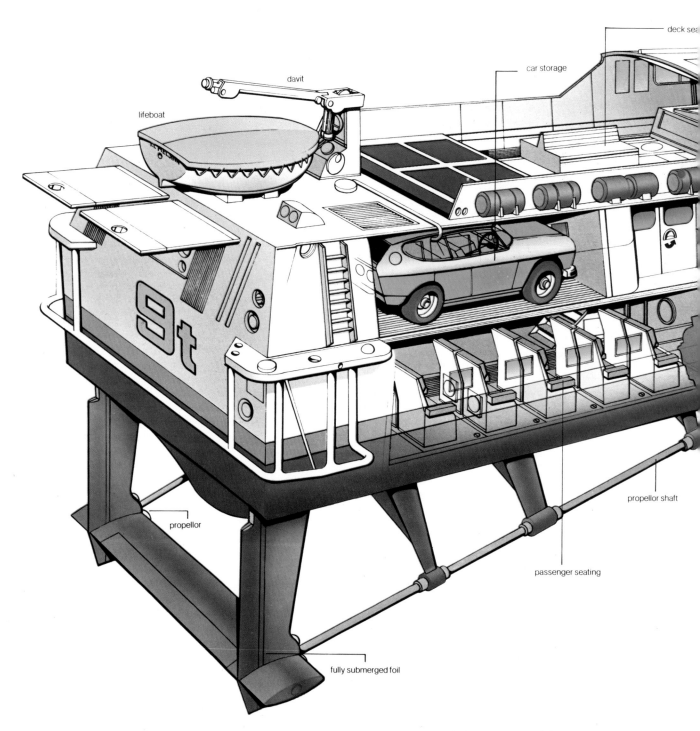

deck sea

car storage

davit

lifeboat

9t

propellor

propellor shaft

passenger seating

fully submerged foil

A hydrofoil boat is analogous in principle to an aircraft. It comprises a boat-shaped hull to which are attached 'wings' or hydrofoils which generate lift as they travel through the water, in the same way that the aerofoil design of the aircraft wing provides lift in the air. When the hydrofoil boat attains speed, the lift provided by the flow of water over the hydrofoil is sufficient to lift the hull entirely clear of the water. Once out of the water, the hull no longer suffers resistance from friction or from waves in rough water, so that higher speeds and a more stable ride can be achieved.

The hydrofoil is not a new idea; a patent was issued to the Frenchman Farcot in 1869. Around 1900 the Italian Forlanini was building successful hydrofoil boats. The Wright brothers experimented with them before their successful aircraft was flown at Kitty Hawk in 1903; Alexander Graham Bell designed one; the Russian designer Alexeyev, and the German Hans von Schertel have been among the most important hydrofoil engineers since World War I.

Since water is several hundred times as dense as air, the hydrofoil can be much smaller than the wing of an

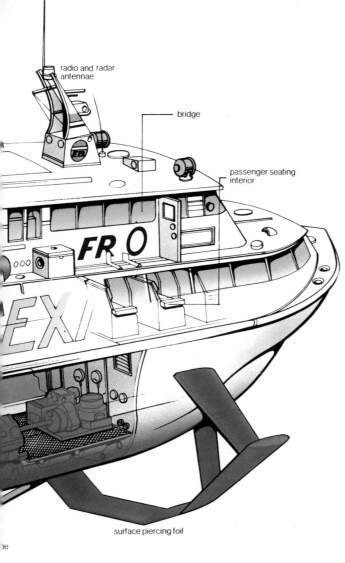

radio and radar
antennae

bridge

passenger seating
interior

FR O

EX

surface piercing foil

A hydrofoil boat is highly manoeuvrable, and can slow down and stop in only three times its length. It creates very little water disturbance and therefore causes little damage to harbours and river banks. Alexander Graham Bell, inventor of the telephone, designed one of the first hydrofoils in 1918-19. Today the Germans and the Italians operate hydrofoil torpedo boats for NATO.

aircraft. There are two principal types of hydrofoil boat design: the fully submerged hydrofoil and the surface-piercing type.

Surface-piercing hydrofoil

This design is by far the most popular for civilian use because of its simplicity. If lift is lost due to the hydrofoil breaking through waves, the craft sinks deeper into the water, thereby immersing more of the foil or foils, which generates more lift. Large numbers of passenger ferries built under licence to designs of the Swiss Supramar company are now in service, and all except the largest of these are of this type.

A 200 ton naval hydrofoil, *Bras D'Or*, built in Canada, has demonstrated that the surface piercing design is suitable for operation on the open sea, where rough water can be expected. Foilborne speeds in

excess of sixty knots have been achieved. The Russians, who are by far the biggest operators of hydrofoils, mostly on lakes and rivers, build several types of shallowly submerged hydrofoil craft, closely related to the surface-piercing type. Examples are the *Kometa*, *Meteor* and *Raketa* types.

Fully submerged hydrofoils

In this type of design only vertical struts pierce the water surface, and changes in lift are effected by changing the angle of attack of the foil to the water. This is achieved by hydraulic or pneumatic cylinders activated by electrical signals from a sonar device pointing ahead of the craft, which reads the oncoming wave height and selects a suitable hydrofoil angle to give the necessary lift.

The principal user of this type of craft is the United States, which has built large naval craft, some having retractable hydrofoils which can swing up out of the water to allow the boat to operate in the conventional way in shallow channels. One of the most successful designs of this type is the *Tucumcari*, built by Boeing. Another system of stabilization, used on smaller craft, uses mechanical sensor-floats on arms ahead of the craft, mechanically linked to the fully submerged foils.

An early variation of the hydrofoil configuration was the 'ladder' type, the more 'rungs' being immersed the greater the lift generated. An early hydrofoil boat of this type was the Bell-Baldwin HD4 which in 1919 attained a speed of sixty knots on the Bras D'Or lakes in Canada. (1 knot=1 nautical mile=6080 ft=1852 m per hour.)

In some designs the large part of the hull weight, usually between 80 and 90%, is supported by a large foil or foils located forward on the hull: in others the large foils are located aft. The remaining hull weight is supported by a smaller foil which can be turned to provide a steering function while the craft is foilborne.

Propulsion

Power units for commercial craft usually consist of marine diesel engines which drive propellers at the end of long inclined shafts. In military craft, sometimes designed for anti-submarine duties towing sonar equipment, and where light weight and high speed are considerations but cost is not, gas turbines are used. Often an entirely separate propulsion system is also fitted for slow speed operation in the conventional hullborne way. Water jets have also been used.

Limitations

Above about fifty knots, hydrofoils have to be specially designed to cope with increased turbulence in the same way that wings of supersonic aircraft are designed to cope with breaking the sound barrier. Hydrofoils will not replace the largest ocean-going vessels for the same reason that limits the practical size of aircraft: the cube-square law. As the size of a hydrofoil (or an aerofoil) increases, its weight increases in cubic increments, while the area available to support the weight only increases in square increments.

THE AIR-CUSHION VEHICLE

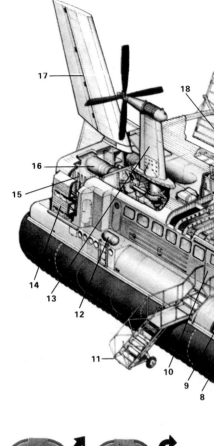

Air cushion vehicles—also known as hovercraft or, in the United States of America, as ground effect machines (GEM)—are vehicles which when in motion are supported by a layer of air, rather than by wheels or other direct means of contact with the ground over which they pass.

This absence of contact with the surface has brought the advantages of both adaptability and speed: the latter is particularly well demonstrated when the ACV is compared with the conventional ship. For example, the world's largest passenger ACV, the 190-ton SR-N4, capable of speeds of nearly 80 knots (150 km/h) and cruises at around 50 knots (90 km/h). The top speed for a crack liner is around 35 knots (65 km/h).

There are a number of reasons why this is so. First, in a conventional ship that area of the hull which is normally submerged is subjected to drag as a result of the viscosity of the water through which it travels. Drag absorbs a good deal of engine power.

Second, wave formations are set up at bow and stern of a ship when it is under way. Again, this wave making process means a drain on the power supply. Although this is less important than drag at low speeds, as speed increases it takes over as the major power wastage problem.

Finally, there are the natural phenomena of currents and of windage on the exposed areas of hull and superstructure, and these may sometimes work adversely.

Considering the first two factors alone, it can be appreciated that the bigger and faster the ship, the larger the amount of energy wasted. There comes a point when the cost of deriving more speed from a ship outweighs the advantages—unless there are special factors like military or research requirements.

Since none of the ACV is immersed it has none of these problems. At low speeds a wave making process is set up, at cruising speeds, however, this disappears. Though the ACV is affected by adverse winds, it is generally faster not only than a conventional vessel of the same size but also larger ships.

In principle the ACV works in the following way. The hull can be thought of as being something like an upturned tea tray with raised edges. If such a structure were placed carefully on the surface of water, a quantity of air would be trapped beneath it, retained by the edges which would now be jutting downwards. If, however, you attempted to propel the tray through the water, the air would escape and the tray would sink. Even if that did not happen, the submerged portions of the edges would be subjected to friction and would set up waves.

The pioneer designers were faced with two problems: how to raise the craft clear of the water, and how to keep the air cushion permanently in place. They overcame the first problem by ducting air into the cushion compartment at pressure a little higher than atmospheric, and the second by arranging a system of air jets around the edge to provide a curtain of air which

slowed down the rate of leakage from the cushion. This system was improved by the addition of a flexible skirt around the edge of the vessel.

It has been calculated that a pressure of only about 60 lb per square foot (300 kg/m²) is required to raise an ACV of 100 tons or more to a height of one foot (30 cm). The pressure required to inflate car tyres is a good deal greater.

Types of ACV

Several variations of the basic ACV principle have been evolved. The simplest is called the air-bearing system. Air is blown through a central orifice in the undersurface and leaks away outwards under the flexible retaining skirt.

The plenum chamber vessel has a concave undersurface, and the cavity forms the upper section of a cushion chamber which is completed by the sea or ground surface; again the air leaks away under the edges.

In the momentum-curtain system a ring of air jets is set around the circumference of the underside of the ACV. The air from these jets is directed downwards and inwards to retain the air cushion. This system has been further developed to include two rows of peripheral jets, one inside the other. The retaining air is blown out through one set, sucked up by the other

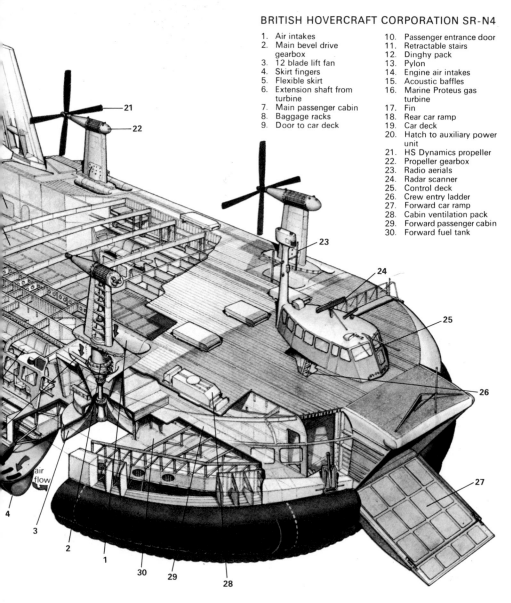

BRITISH HOVERCRAFT CORPORATION SR-N4

1. Air intakes
2. Main bevel drive gearbox
3. 12 blade lift fan
4. Skirt fingers
5. Flexible skirt
6. Extension shaft from turbine
7. Main passenger cabin
8. Baggage racks
9. Door to car deck
10. Passenger entrance door
11. Retractable stairs
12. Dinghy pack
13. Pylon
14. Engine air intakes
15. Acoustic baffles
16. Marine Proteus gas turbine
17. Fin
18. Rear car ramp
19. Car deck
20. Hatch to auxiliary power unit
21. HS Dynamics propeller
22. Propeller gearbox
23. Radio aerials
24. Radar scanner
25. Control deck
26. Crew entry ladder
27. Forward car ramp
28. Cabin ventilation pack
29. Forward passenger cabin
30. Forward fuel tank

Left: the British Hovercraft Corporation's SR-N4 is the largest ACV in service, at over 160 tons. Several of this type are operated regularly across the English Channel. The four rear-mounted gas turbines each drive one lift fan and one propeller, geared together: the front ones are driven by long extension shafts.
Below: the Voyageur ACV was developed for use in Canada, where the wide variety of terrain, including lakes frozen in winter, makes it ideal. Its 25 ton capacity compares well with cargo aircraft.

after it has done its job, and then recirculated. This makes for greater efficiency, since it slows down the rate of air escape.

ACV propulsion systems have also been varied. The most popular for large vessels has been the airscrew or propeller. In the earliest machines, the fans that provided lift also drove air through a system of ducts to the stern where it was ejected for propulsion. In the SR-N4, the four engines that drive the lift fans also drive external airscrews for propulsion. In many other types, however, the lift and propulsion systems are separately powered. Some ACVs have been fitted with water propellers but this limits their use to the water.

The problems of steering an ACV are very similar to those of steering an aircraft. As the ACV has no contact with sea or land, there is a danger of drift during

THE BATHYSCAPHE

turns. The helmsman overcomes this by banking, or tilting, his machine like an aircraft. He does so by reducing the pressure from the air jets on the side which he wants to dip. Directional control is exerted by varying the power of the airscrew, by using aero rudders, or with both systems at once.

Development

The air cushion principle has fascinated designers for many years. Pioneering attempts at its use were made as far back as the 1930s, in both the United States and Finland. It was not until after World War II, however, that the real breakthrough came.

The inventor of the first successful ACV was Britain's C S Cockerell. Trained as an engineer and in electronics, he later turned his attention to the problems of boat design. He tried at first to retain an air cushion under a boat by fitting hinged flaps at the bow and stern of his craft between side keels. Except for the hinging, it was the same principle as the tea tray example. Finding this technique to be ineffective, he replaced the flaps with sheets of water pumped vertically downwards. Air containment was still not very efficient, and finally he struck on the idea of using peripheral air jets for the purpose.

The world's first hovercraft, the SR-NI, was unveiled in 1959 when it travelled from the Isle of Wight to mainland England. Only a few weeks later it crossed the English Channel in two hours, and in 1965 the world's first regular passenger service was set up between the Isle of Wight and the mainland. Now a fleet of SR-N4s carries passengers and cars regularly to and from France, by 1975 capturing 29 per cent of the total traffic.

Because the air cushion acts not only as a form of support but also as an effective spring, the modern ACV can cope with waves of up to ten feet (3 m) or operate over rough ground. It has been used for military purposes by the USA in Vietnam and elsewhere in the Far East. It was even employed on one occasion to carry a British expedition to the upper reaches of the Amazon.

The advantages of this type of craft in naval warfare are considerable. It is not only speedy, but the larger types can deliver torpedoes and other missiles with telling effect. At the same time, since they are not in contact with the sea themselves, they are immune to torpedo attack; the missile simply passes harmlessly beneath them. This however presupposes that an enemy submarine can find them. The insulation of the air cushion makes it difficult for submarine listening gear to pick up the sound of the ACV's propulsion system.

The United States Navy is planning a 10,000 ton version for the late 1970s which will carry jet fighters of the vertical take-off type. For both civil and military purposes, the ACV has the advantage that it can make the transition from sea to shore with relative ease. No expensive docking facilities are required.

For a long time underwater research into marine life and the nature of the ocean floor was limited by the equipment available. The development of the aqualung [scuba] has enabled a diver to dive to a maximum depth of about 165 ft (50m). Piccard's invention, in the late 1940s, of a diving vessel—the bathyscaphe—designed to withstand high pressure enabled the scientist to descend several miles below the surface of the sea. The name is derived from the Greek *bathys* meaning 'deep' and *scaphos* which means 'ship'.

The bathyscaphe is constructed of two main parts, a large, usually hull-shaped float which is a lighter-than-water container filled with fuel, and a spherical steel cabin suspended below it. In the float, the petrol is divided among several compartments, and the craft is trimmed by the movement of quantities of iron shot. This ballast is situated in hoppers inside the float and secured by electro-magnets.

The sphere is the control centre of the craft; it houses the crew, the controls and any research equipment. As the sphere must withstand great pressures, about eight tons per sq in (1240 bar) at a depth of six miles (10,000 m), the wall thickness varies from four to seven inches (10 cm to 18 cm). Because the bathyscaphe is a scientific research craft, the two man crew must be able to look out at their surroundings. The sphere is therefore equipped with portholes and great care must be taken to ensure that the transparent material—which is usually Perspex [Plexiglas]— is seated in the surrounding metal so that the seal is perfect. At the pressures encountered, even a fine jet of water spouting into the sphere would do considerable damage. For this reason the ports are constructed like a cone with the narrow point sliced off. They are glued into the sockets and inserted narrow end first into a matching hole, so that mounting pressure merely pushes the port more securely into its bed. Similar ingenuity is required to stop leakages at the points where electrical conduits pass through the walls of the sphere, with the additional problem that the cables will flex when the craft is being used. The epoxy resin adhesive Araldite has been found to be an effective fixative and sealant but experiments are going on with even tougher substances developed in the United States space programme.

The typical bathyscaphe sphere holds two men and provides air at normal atmospheric pressure so that there is no need for the crew to decompress after a dive. Air cylinders are housed inside the sphere and the supply usually lasts for about 24 hours. The sphere also contains the controls for the ballast and any external grabs as well as sonar equipment and television monitor.

Operating the bathyscaphe

When the bathyscaphe is on the surface and preparing for a dive, some of the compartments in the float are filled with air. For diving, these compartments are flooded with sea water. As the vessel sinks, the outside of the

62

The Aluminaut *is fifty feet long and is designed to cruise at a depth of three miles.*

float is subjected to increasing pressure. The bottoms of the compartments which contain petrol are open to the sea and the pressure of the water slightly compresses the lighter liquid ensuring that at all times the pressure inside the float is the same as that outside. For this reason it is possible to construct the float of much lighter gauge metal than the sphere. Another effect of the compression of the petrol is that the deeper the bathyscaphe goes, the denser the petrol becomes until its density is even more than water. This makes the craft heavier and it sinks much faster. To control this, the crew can release small amounts of the ballast. The bathyscaphe is kept clear of the sea bed both by trimming the ballast so that the craft achieves neutral buoyancy at the desired level, and also by means of the guide chain.

This is a very simple device: simply a length of chain which hangs below the vessel. When the end touches the sea bed the bathyscaphe is lightened by the weight of the chain which has grounded. The bathyscaphe then slows up and the weight of chain lying on the bottom reaches the right level the craft will have

achieved neutral buoyancy. The chain also aids the stability of the vessel by acting as a drag line. Mobility on the bottom is limited: a massive structure is required to take two men to great depths and there is little room for anything more than small motors and electrical power packs. In practise, the crews of bathyscaphes frequently use undersea currents to help in the work of propulsion.

To return to the surface the crew switches off the electromagnets, the rest of the shot empties away, and the light petrol 'balloons' the craft to the surface. In the event of a power failure exactly the same thing happens. This fail-safe system is augmented by other bunkers, containing heavy scrap, which can also be emptied, and by the jettisoning of some pieces of heavy equipment secured by electromagnets.

Development

Similar spheres called bathyspheres were used for very deep diving before the advent of the bathyscaphe after

63

AMPHIBIANS

World War II. These had the disadvantages of being suspended from a surface vessel by cables. The inventor of the bathyscaphe was Professor Auguste Piccard. Famous in the 1930s for his ballooning exploits, he decided to apply analogous ideas to deep sea exploration. The function of the float is the same as that of the balloon's gas bag. Ascent and descent in both are dependent on ballast trimming and, to some extent, on a drag cable. To enable the crew of either to breathe air at sea level pressure a self-contained air supply must be carried.

Piccard's work was supported initially by the Belgian National Foundation for Scientific Research (FRNS). Hence his famous balloon was called the FRNS1. His first bathyscaphe was called the FRNS 2 and proved beyond doubt that his ideas worked. However, it was the *Trieste*, named after the city from which his backers came, which provided his greatest triumph. Piloted by his son Jacques and a colleague, this vessel carried out a whole series of dives to ever greater depths, culminating in the present world record: a dive to 35,00 ft (11,000 m)—Mount Everest is only 29,000 ft (8800 m)—in 1960 in the Marianas Trench in the Pacific Ocean. Since then the *Trieste* was successfully used to find the remains of the sunken nuclear submarine *Thresher* and bring some of the wreckage to the surface.

Development work is now going on in France (FRNS III), the United States (the advanced *Trieste* II) and in the Soviet Union (the B-II, scheduled for launching in the late 1970s).

Amphibious vehicles, or amphibians, can move both on land and in water under their own power. Development of amphibians for military and pleasure use has produced many different technical approaches from the military DUKW to the American home-made swamp buggies.

The first true amphibious vehicle was probably the French Fournier of 1906, which combined a boat-type hull with an automobile chassis. A shaft transmission drove both the rear axle and a single propeller. Modern pleasure amphibians still follow this basic pattern.

Most famous of all amphibians, and still one of the most versatile vehicles in use, is the American built General Motors Corporation DUKW ('Duplex Universal Karrier, Wheeled'). First built in 1942 and primarily used for ship-to-shore transport, it is based on a truck chassis and has a six cylinder 4.4 litre engine driving all six wheels. All wheels steer on land, and on water they assist a rudder. A single propeller is driven through a transfer case—a gearbox which enables it to be switched in and out. The six and a half ton amphibian can achieve 50 mile/h (80 km/h) on land and 6 mile/h (10 km/h) on water. Production ceased in 1945, but 'ducks' are still in use with armed forces all over the world.

Another major class of amphibian is known in the USA as the LVT, short for Landing Vehicle, Tracked. The LVT, nicknamed the 'Buffalo', started as a rescue vehicle. It was designed in 1932 by Donald Roebling for use in the Florida swamplands and later developed as a military vehicle for carrying men and materials over rivers or on sea-borne landings.

Right: the American 'Deep Quest' vehicle. A similar device was involved in the salvage of a hydrogen bomb which was lost in the Mediterranean in 1966.
Far right: tracked landing vehicles in Operation Deep Furrow, Mediterranean, 1971. They weigh about 38 tons (38,500 kg) when fully laden.

The LVT is driven on both land and water by tracks equipped with W shaped protruberances (grousers) to give greater thrust. Buffers set between the driving wheels support the tracks and prevent them from being forced inwards by water pressure, thus giving a greater effective driving surface.

Later models were fitted with Cadillac engines and automatic gearboxes. Current LVTs have side screens along the top run of the tracks and a cowl over the front of them, so that water carried forward by the top of the tracks is directed toward the rear again and so contributes to the forward thrust. Another gain in thrust comes from grilles at the back which channel the wash straight behind the vehicle. LVTs can cope with rocky beaches and heavy surf with equal ease.

During the Second World War, it was often necessary to convert a military vehicle into an amphibian, and Duplex Drive was devised by Nicholas Straussler to allow tanks to float into battle. The DD Sherman was so used on D Day in 1944. A platform of mild steel is welded round the waterproofed tank's hull and a raised canvas or plastic screen is erected round it to give buoyancy. This is generally supported by a series of rubber tubes inflated from cylinders of compressed air carried on the tank's superstructure.

Small propellers were originally driven by the tracks on early models but the vulnerability of propellers on land led to the increasingly widespread use of water jet propulsion. A ducted propeller sucks in water from under the body and squirts it through steering valves at the back. Russia leads in this field but the armies of

Above: the LVTs in the previous picture, coming ashore. They carry 25 to 30 people, and they are about 30 feet (10 m) long.

many nations now have troop carriers and reconnaisance vehicles driven by water jets.

Flotation screens are still used on a few military vehicles like the Vickers 37 ton tank and the Ferret Mk V Scout car, but most modern designers prefer either to forgo amphibious qualities or to build true amphibians.

Developments in armour contruction enable modern tanks to be lighter than their predecessors but just as well protected, so it is not difficult to produce light tanks that can float unassisted. A prime example is the Russian PT-76 amphibious tank powered by a water jet.

The standard Russian technique allows tanks to submerge to cross rivers. This type of amphibian was pioneered during World War II by the Americans and Germans, and submersible tanks were to have been used in Hitler's abortive invasion of Britain.

They have snorkels (air tubes) extending to the surface, bringing air to both crew and engine. The French AMX30 tank has a 15 ft (4.6 m) long tube, wide enough to allow the commander to stand in the top and relay instructions to his submerged crew.

The air tube principle was also used on the British Austin Champ jeep. It had an extendable air pipe leading to the carburettor on the waterproofed engine. True amphibious jeeps were the World War II Volkswagen Schwimmwagen and the GPA (General Purpose Amphibious') version of the American Jeep, which is still popular.

On the GPA Jeep, the watertight hull was constructed separately from the basic chassis to make replacement easy. The propeller was fitted into a duct for protection and was driven by a separate shaft mounted alongside the main drive to the rear wheels. The vehicle weighed more than a conventional Jeep but could still reach 50 mile/h (80 km/h) on the road.

FISHING AND WHALING VESSELS

For 20,000 years man has used hooks, lines, nets and traps to catch fish and the sea is still harvested mainly by hunting. A fisherman using primitive methods from a reed boat or dugout canoe, as they still do in some parts of the world, can produce up to 3 tons of fish in a year. Although modern fishing fleets employ methods and equipment that are not very different in principle, the use of mechanical power, electronics and refrigeration now enables each fisherman to produce fifty or a hundred times that amount. This result is achieved, however, by designing and building vessels which, size for size, are more expensive than any other except ships of war.

Purse seining

The principal method of capture is the purse seine. After detecting a shoal of fish, the skipper manoeuvres his ship, taking into account wind, current and the speed and direction of the shoal, so as to surround the fish with a wall of fine netting suspended from floats, which is fed out over the stern of the ship as it travels. The net is then drawn together at the bottom, and after most of it has been hauled back on board, and provided the fish have not escaped meanwhile, they are scooped or pumped on to the deck. Some purse seines are hundreds of yards in circumference and, if there is the slightest breeze, it is necessary to take steps to prevent the ship becoming entangled in the net. American purse seiners carry a powerful motor skiff which is used as a tug; European fisherman equip their vessels with devices to produce sideways thrust, such as propellers working in transverse tunnels in the hull, or rotating cylinder rudders.

The skippers know from experience which sea areas are most likely to yield good catches, according to season; they may get up-to the-minute information from colleagues over the radio-telephone, and other indications are water temperature and animal life. Actual shoals may be detected at distances of a few miles by the behaviour of birds or, at night, by phosphorescence in the water. Aerial reconnaissance, using low-light-level TV at night, has sometimes been used. When the ship has closed the range to about 1000 yards (900 m) sonar may be employed to maintain contact with the shoal.

Trawling

Shoaling species can also be captured with a mid-water trawl towed at $\frac{1}{2}$ to 5 knots (nautical miles per hour—1 nautical mile per hour is about 1.15 mph) by a single vessel or a pair of vessels. Paired mid-water trawling, where the net is towed between two ships, is used in confined waters. Single-boat mid-water trawls, to be effective, must be so large and delicate, and are so slow to manoeuvre, that their successful use depends upon the skipper having precise knowledge of the position of the net in relation to the sea bed and the surface.

This is done by attaching vertical echo-sounders to the trawl; the information is telemetered to the ship by cable or acoustic beam. A forward-looking sonar may also be mounted on the trawl to enable the skipper to observe the shoal as the net approaches.

Other methods include gill nets (so called because they catch the fish by the gills as they try to swim through) and pole fishing (rod and line); the twenty or

Right: a mixed catch nears the ramp of a stern trawler. The net is divided in two so that half the the catch is saved if a net is holed.
Far right: modern fishing vessels are equipped with sonar devices for finding shoals of fish. The bottom half of the picture is what the sonar reading looks like.

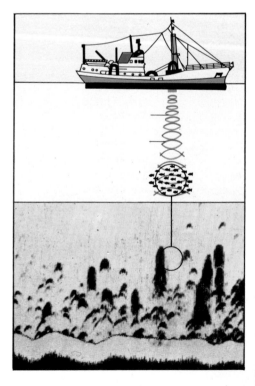

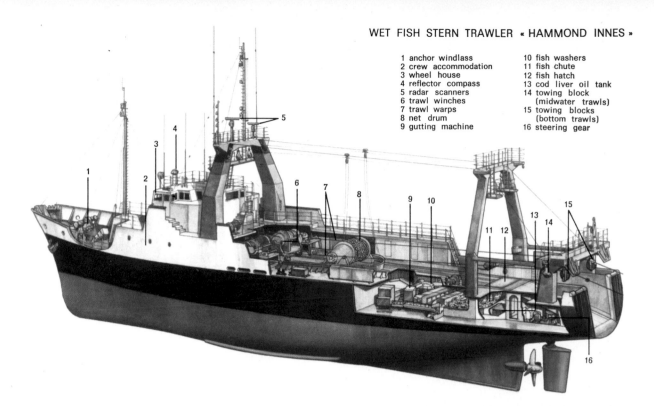

1 anchor windlass
2 crew accommodation
3 wheel house
4 reflector compass
5 radar scanners
6 trawl winches
7 trawl warps
8 net drum
9 gutting machine
10 fish washers
11 fish chute
12 fish hatch
13 cod liver oil tank
14 towing block (midwater trawls)
15 towing blocks (bottom trawls)
16 steering gear

thirty fisherman formerly employed on a pole-fishing tuna vessel may nowadays be replaced by mechanical robots. When the tuna shoals are dispersed, floating baited lines 75 miles (120 km) or more in length may be employed.

Non-shoaling species can also be caught by baited hooks, on lines up to 20 miles (32 km) long laid on the sea bed, but the most important method of capturing these fish is by using the otter trawl. A trawl is a tapering bag of netting towed behind the ship, in this case on the sea bed. The vertical opening of the mouth is maintained by floats on the headline and weights on the footrope, the lateral opening by two otter boards, wooden or steel kites running on their edges on the sea bed, one attached to each side of the net by wire rope bridles.

Bottom trawling is carried out in depths down to 500 fathoms (900 m) or more (one fathom is six feet or 1.8 m), but the length of the two warps or towing cables attached to the otter boards is usually 2½ or 3 times the depth of water. The trawl is hauled up to the surface by winches which in the biggest vessels may use 500 horsepower motors.

A very effective method on a smooth sea bed is bottom seining. A trawl net, without otter boards, is attached to two towing ropes up to 2 miles (3 km) long; ropes and net are paid out on the sea bed in a great circle and, as the ropes are winched in, they move closer together and shepherd the fish into the path of the advancing net.

Fishing aids

Important aids in trawling and bottom seining include warp tension meters which measure the loads on the towing cables and, among other things, give warning of the net coming fast on an obstruction; the vertical echo-sounder, some versions of which can detect a single fish within a few feet of the sea bed in 100 fathoms (180 m) of water; and radio navigation devices such as LORAN C and DECCA, which are used in conjunction with large-scale charts on which is

Above top: a wet fish stern trawler, the Hammond Innes. *The catch is gutted and washed by machines, then kept at a temperature of 0°C (32°F). 'Wet fish' means that the fish are not frozen on board.*
Above: the covered quay at a British fishing port. Here the catch is auctioned off.

67

*Right, top to bottom:
longlining is used mainly
for tuna fishing, and uses a
line many miles long with
baited branches; stern
ramp trawling is more
efficient than side
trawling as the net is
easier to handle; the stick
held dip net uses lights on
one side of the boat to
attract the fish. The
lights are then put out and
lit on the the other side
causing the fish to swim
into the net; the Pacific
shrimp boat uses two beam
nets towed from outrigger
booms. The nets trawl
along the bottom.*

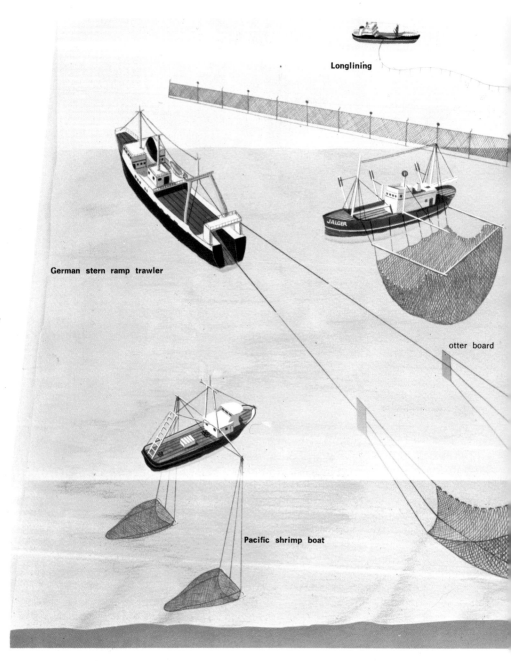

Longlining

German stern ramp trawler

otter board

Pacific shrimp boat

*Right: a stern trawler
returning to port. Drawn
up to the sides of the ship
near the stern are the
otter boards, which act as
rudders to keep the net
open.*

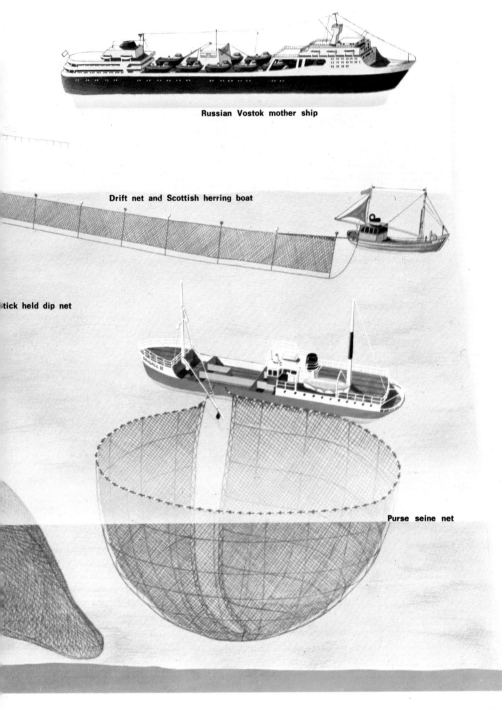

Russian Vostok mother ship

Drift net and Scottish herring boat

tick held dip net

Purse seine net

Left, top to bottom: a Russian Vostok factory ship of 43,500 tons carries its own fleet of 14 catcher vessels of 66 tons each. The catch is frozen on board; the Scottish herring boat uses a drift net about three miles long. Small fish swim through but others are caught by the gills; the purse seine net is shot from the side of the boat and closed around a shoal of fish discovered by means of sonar.

recorded hard-won information on sea-bed obstructions, rough ground and currents, and also on the fishing tactics appropriate to the area and season. An active trawling simulator has been developed on which aspiring trawl skippers may learn to interpret the information from their fishing aids and to manoeuvre ship and trawl to best advantage.

Some trawl nets are longer than the biggest trawlers, which are about 350 feet (100 m) overall; a mid-water trawl may be big enough to envelop St Paul's Cathedral, London; a purse seine may be 1000 fathoms (1800 m) long and 100 fathoms (180 m) deep. The use of big seines only became feasible with the introduction of hydraulically driven rubber-lined open sheaves, called power blocks, to haul the net on board. Trawl nets used to be hauled on board by hand but can now be wound on to powered drums or reels.

Storage and processing

Once the catch is on board, it is processed and stored according to its intended market and the distance from port. A single haul of herring or anchovy may be 100 tons or more but this type of fish is usually destined for reduction to edible oils and animal feeding stuffs—about 40% of the world catch of marine fish is utilized thus—and may simply be stored below in bulk without further treatment. Fish intended for human consumption, if it is to be landed within, say, one to fifteen days of the time of capture (depending on species, market, season and climate) is normally stored in boxes or on shelves and spoilage is retarded by mixing it with melting crushed ice, or by storing it in tanks of refrigerated seawater.

Crabs and lobsters are caught by baited traps, and also by trawls, at depths down to 200 fathoms (360 m). Smaller crustaceans are caught by trawls and dredges, as are molluscs living below water mark. Hand-gathering is still employed as a method for harvesting molluscs in the intertidal zone but there also exist ship-mounted power dredges fitted with hydraulic digging jets and with jet pumps to deliver the catch continuously on board. Two men so equipped can produce a ton of edible protein in an hour's fishing.

Large distant-water trawlers and tuna clippers make voyages of many weeks or even a few months' duration. Some cod is still split and salted at sea and subsequently dried ashore for consumption in Mediterranean, African and Latin American countries, but most of the distant-water catch is now quick-frozen at sea and stored on board at temperatures of —20 °F (—30 °C) or lower. Tuna may be frozen in tanks through which refrigerated brine is circulated; whole fish are also frozen in cold-air-blast tunnels, or in vertical-plate contact-freezers between parallel, hollow, refrigerated metal plates. Fillets are usually frozen at sea into regular blocks of 25 to 100 lb (11 to 45 kg) in horizontal-plate contact-freezers, the blocks are destined for reprocessing on shore into fish fingers [fish sticks] or standard frozen portions.

Trawlers equipped to freeze the catch on board are usually of the modern high-freeboard shelter-deck stern-fishing type which is fast replacing the low-freeboard, open-deck, single-decked side-fishing trawler which evolved from traditional sail-powered fishing vessel types in the nineteenth century. Mother-ships, with attendant catching vessels, are used in some fisheries; the largest is the Russian *Vostock* of 43,500 tons; she carries on board fourteen catchers each of which is 60 ft (18 m) long and equipped with a 600 horsepower engine. Some factory ships produce fish meal—dried ground fish—for animal feeding stuffs; some are canneries.

Before it is chilled or frozen the catch will have been sorted, washed and — depending upon species and market—it may be bled, gutted and beheaded, or split, (filleted). Some fish livers contain vitamins A and D and are retained for further processing when the fish is gutted. Filleting is the removal of the edible flesh from the skeleton in one or two large pieces. All of these processes can now be carried out mechanically. Machines for gutting and filleting are extremely complex, not only because of the anatomical problems but also because they must adjust automatically to the size of each individual fish. Some Japanese factory ships are equipped with machines to process the fish flesh into *surimi*, a frozen minced or ground product which is the raw material for *kamaboko* or fish jelly and other manufactured foods.

Whaling

The technology of whaling begins with the Stone Age weapons of early polar people. Explorers discovered the

North American Eskimos to be proficient at killing whales and using the blubber and its oil for light, heat and food. The Eskimos hunted whales from small skin boats. When a whale was sighted as it came to the surface for air, 'blowing', the Eskimos threw harpoons, attached to lines made of skin, into the whale. Then they were taken for a fast ride in their small boats until the animal gradually tired and could be brought close enough to be killed with spears or lances. Natives of the Aleutian Islands and Northern Japan were thought to have used poisoned spear tips with out a line. They waited for the wounded whale to die and float to the surface before securing it and bringing it back to shore.

The first whaling of commercial importance was done by the Basques in the Bay of Biscay around the 11th century. As more uses were found for whale oil, many countries began competing in the lucrative business and by the 19th century stocks of the slow-moving *right* whales were becoming depleted.

Whale meat and blubber deteriorate rapidly; early whaling expeditions were hampered by the need to return catches to shore stations for processing. In the 1760s however, tryworks (brick ovens used to convert whale blubber to oil) appeared on American vessels and made voyages of four years and more possible.

The hand-thrown harpoon was developed and modified until, in 1864, the Norwegian Swend Foyn invented a gun to fire harpoons with explosive heads. Heavy line ran from the harpoon through a spring tackle to absorb shock and was controlled by a steam winch. These heavy guns, mounted on the foredeck of faster, steam-powered boats, made it possible to hunt the elusive *fin*, *sei* and *blue* whales.

New techniques, and consequently larger catches, encouraged the development of massive shore stations where entire carcasses could be processed. The oil formed the base of soap, perfume, glycerine and varnish. A substance called *spermaceti*, which comes from a cavity in the head of sperm whales, was widely used in the manufacture of candles. (The 'candle power' unit of illumination was based on the illuminating power of candles made from this material.) *Baleen*, from plates in the mouths of whales, and misleadingly called whalebone, was much in demand for the manufacture of stays and corsets.

Factory ships

At its peak in the 19th century, the whaling industry was highly competitive, and fishing rights and sovereignty encouraged the Norwegians to develop offshore floating factories. These in turn developed into modern factory ships, independent of land bases.

In *pelagic* (performed on the open sea), or floating factory ship whaling in the 20th century, a whaling expedition may consist of a factory ship (the processing station) complete with laboratory and hospital, a fleet of whale boats called catcher boats, buoy boats for towing the dead whales back to the factory ship, and even helicopters for sighting whales. Supplies and fuel are delivered to the fleet by a tanker, which also takes the processed oil back to port.

Hunting

As stocks of whales have become seriously depleted (some species are almost extinct and are now protected), finding a group, or *pod*, of whales can be extremely difficult. Conventional aircraft were tried at one time but helicopters have been found to be more effective. Sonar has also been used with some success. Other ultrasonic devices are sometimes employed to frighten whales into flight and exhaustion. It is still the lookout man on the catcher boat, however, who usually makes the sighting of a surfacing whale.

Catcher boats are approximately 200 feet (61 m) long, capable of 18 knots and designed for quick turning. A bow gun, mounted on the raised foredeck, fires 6 foot (2 m) harpoons made of soft metal and weighing 120 pounds. The harpoons carry an explosive device, which is fused to detonate seconds after impact. Several hits are often required to kill a whale although the more humane electric harpoons which stun or kill a whale immediately are now widely used. The dead whale is winched to the side of the boat and compressed air is forced into its stomach to keep it afloat and an identifying flag is attached. Radio signal emitters are frequently attached to enable the buoy boat or the catcher boat to locate and round up the drifting whales. It is not uncommon for a catcher boat to cover more than 100 miles (160 km) in a day.

Processing

When the dead whales are towed to the factory ship, they are manoeuvred to the whale slipway—a large hole through which the whale is pulled from the sea to the main deck by steel claws and winches. Because decomposition sets in so quickly, all whales are processed within 36 hours. Giant factory ships are therefore equipped to handle as many as 12 whales a day. Blubber is flensed (stripped) lengthwise in sections, minced and put in high pressure steam cookers. The oil is then purified in a centrifuge. Lemmers (the workmen who butcher whales) separate the flesh from the bone, which is cut up and, because it is oily and porous, pressure-cooked for oil extraction; the residue is ground and bagged as bone meal. The flesh not used for human consumption is processed for oil and the remaining solids are kiln-dried and sold as animal food. In less than an hour, a 100 ton blue whale can be fully processed.

Edible flesh is frozen, canned or reduced to meat extract (whale meat is popular in Japan). Sometimes the fresh meat is transferred to freezer ships for faster distribution. The purified oil is held until collection in the lower tank deck. When oil is to be transferred it must first be heated so that it will pass through pumps to a tanker. In poor weather it is difficult for two large ships to manoeuvre to transfer freight, and dead whales are frequently secured to the side of the factory ship to serve as fenders.

Modern whaling

Modern fleets rely on advanced equipment, including depth recorders and radar, to locate whales. Most whaling ships have underwater rangefinders and bearing indicators which provide continuous information on the whale's position relative to the whaleboat. At close range they can even warn crews that a whale is about to surface.

Despite the advanced technology of modern operations, however, a much smaller number of whales are taken per fleet per day than were taken by comparatively primitive whaling operations in earlier times. This is because centuries of whale-hunting has taken a severe toll. The whale's gestation period is a year or more and this factor makes replenishment of depleted herds slow; the Antarctic grounds are virtually exhausted and other areas are endangered. The International Whaling Commission was established in 1946 with the aim of exploitation without extermination. It acts in an advisory capacity on behalf of member nations, and not all whaling countries belong. The Commission pools statistics and sets limits, and has defined a whale unit, called the Blue Whale Unit (BWU) after the largest whale, so that limits can be easily interpreted. In this system, for example, one blue whale is taken to equal two fin whales, two and half humpback whales or six sei whales. The International Whaling Commission prevents the taking of right and grey whales and all females with calves; minimum sizes are fixed and the whaling season is limited.

PROPULSION

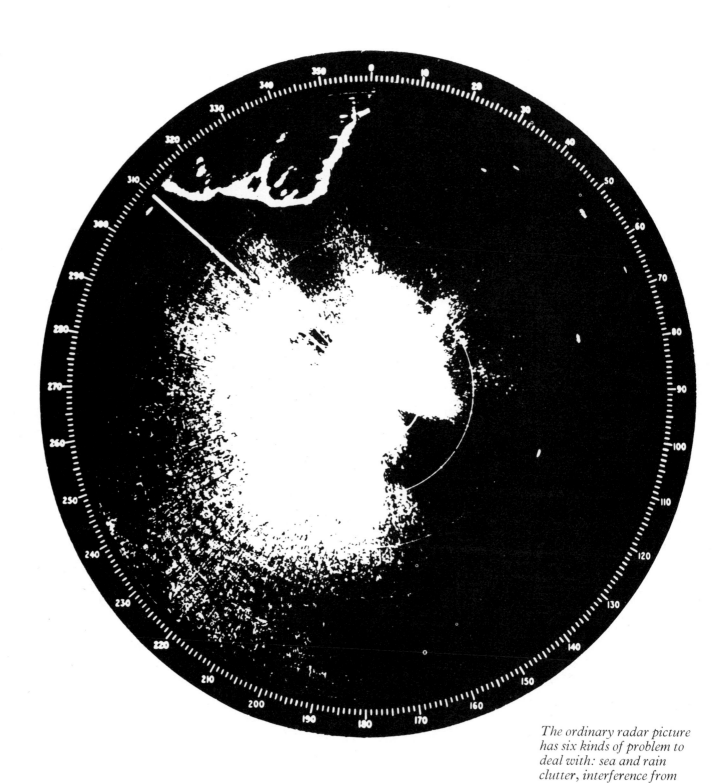

The ordinary radar picture has six kinds of problem to deal with: sea and rain clutter, interference from other ships' radar, receiver noise from the ship's own radar, weak echoes and small echoes. Some of these can be dealt with by manual adjustment of controls, but this must be skilled

72

AND NAVIGATION

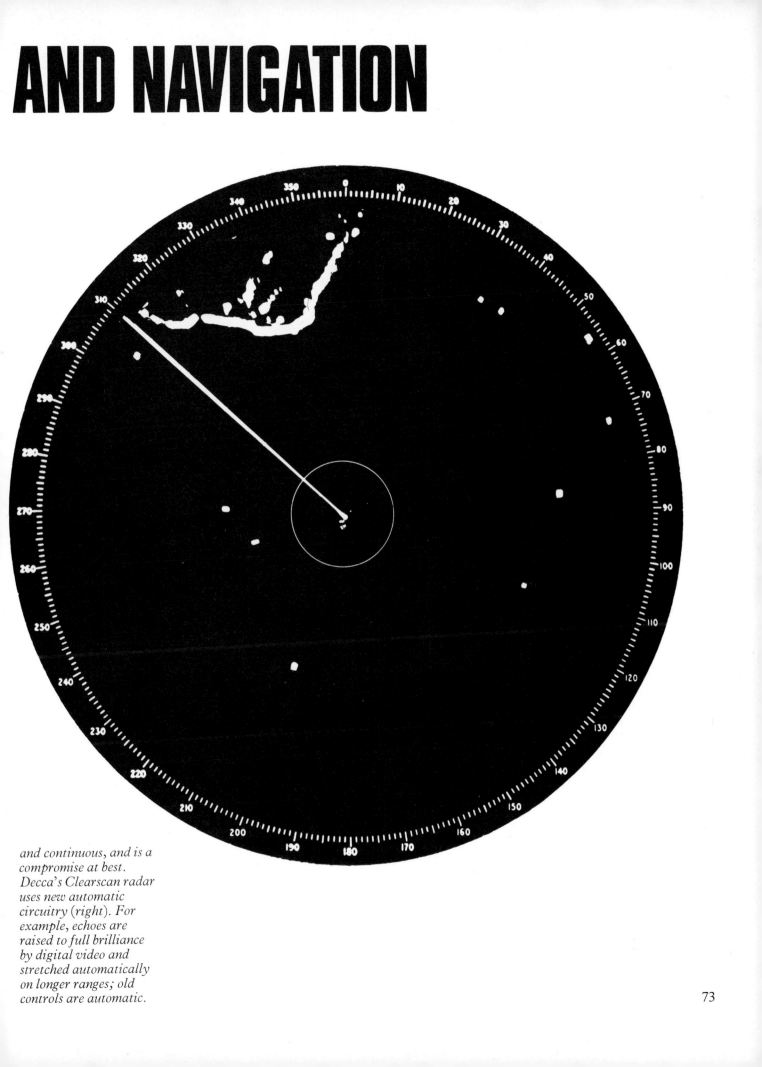

and continuous, and is a
compromise at best.
Decca's Clearscan radar
uses new automatic
circuitry (right). For
example, echoes are
raised to full brilliance
by digital video and
stretched automatically
on longer ranges; old
controls are automatic.

THE MARINE PROPELLER

The propeller, or screw, has been used in ships since about 1850. In its various forms the propeller remains the most efficient method for converting the power developed by a ship's machinery into the necessary thrust to push the vessel through the water.

The propeller works by accelerating the water passing through it, exerting a forward thrust by the reaction from the increase in momentum of the accelerated flow. This momentum is increased by giving either a low increase in speed to a large mass of water (large, slow-running propellers), or a high increase in speed to a small mass of water (small, fast-running propellers). The former represents the most efficient means of propulsion while the latter is less efficient, corresponding to what is commonly understood as jet propulsion.

The flow of water into the propeller is very significantly affected by the shape of the hull immediately ahead of it. In moving forward the ship drags along some of the surrounding water so that the relative speed of advance of the propeller through the water is actually less than the ship's speed. This field of flow created by the ship forward of the propeller is called the wake field. In addition, the axial speed of the water varies across the propeller 'disc' so that each blade in rotating will alternately pass through regions of high-and low-speed water. In general, when the blade is in the top of the aperture (at the 11 o'clock position) the relative water speed will be at its lowest and when the blade is in the bottom of the aperture the water speed will be at its highest. As a result the forces developed by the blades are cyclic in nature, fluctuating about the mean value and giving rise to problems with vibration, strength and cavitation.

Cavitation

A propeller blade acts in a similar way to an aircraft wing in that a section through a blade has an aerofoil shape. The passage of the water sets up a pressure reduction on the forward side of the blades and a pressure increase on the aft side of the blades. The largest contribution to the propeller thrust comes from the pressure reduction, and if the pressure at any point falls to the pressure at which water vaporizes, then cavities of vapour are created in the water. This phenomenon is termed cavitation and can be detrimental to the efficient operation of the propeller. The subsequent collapse of the cavities can also cause

Below: a variable-pitch device for a marine propeller. This design eliminates the need for high-pressure seals on the hydraulic mechanism by using pumps turning with the shaft.

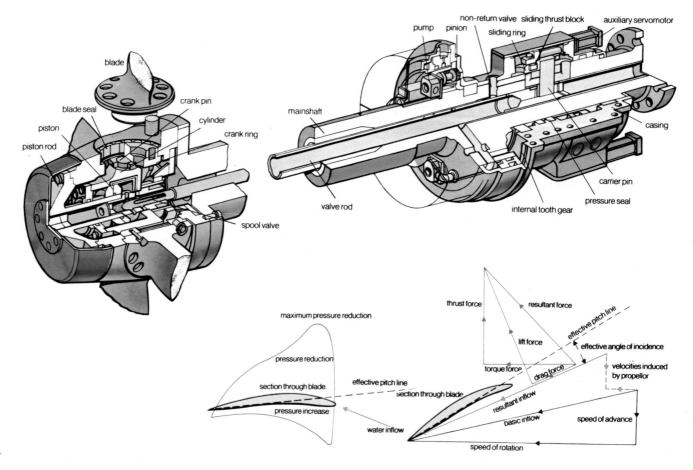

Left: the world's largest marine propeller weighs 72 tons. It is fitted to the 386,000 ton tanker Ioannis Coloctronis. Below: casting a six-bladed propeller like the one above may involve pouring more than 100 tons of a high-tensile non-ferrous alloy such as manganese bronze. Such a large amount is necessary because extensive machining of the finished casting must be done to obtain good balance and precise shape. The mould will probably be made of sand in a cement bond.

noise, erosion of the blade surfaces, and increased vibration.

The risk of cavitation is the main reason that a marine propeller differs from its airscrew equivalent in that it has much wider blades. A wide blade helps to restrict the level of the pressure reduction and so reduce the amount of cavitation. Nevertheless, because of the variations in water speed into the propeller it is often impossible to eliminate it completely.

Design

The objective of the designer is to produce a propeller that will convert the ship's power into thrust at the highest possible efficiency, the propeller being strong enough to withstand all the forces involved without causing blade fracture and shaped in such a way that the harmful effects of cavitation are avoided. As such the propeller must be 'tailor made' for the ship that it is to propel using a design procedure that is a blend of theory, model experiment and experience.

A very important requirement of any propeller design is to ensure that the ship's power is converted into thrust at the prescribed rate of revolutions, and this is dependent to a large extent on the propeller pitch. The pitch is the distance that the propeller would theoretically move forward in one complete revolution if

Above top: the auxiliary motor on a sailboat projects through a well in the hull.
Above: a small water-jet propulsion unit is shown cutaway so that the pump drive shaft and the impeller can be seen.
Water is drawn in through the grill at the bottom, and expelled through a movable discharge nozzle (left).

it were working in a solid substance. However, due to the fluid nature of water the propeller actually moves forward somewhat less than the pitch.

As the pitch of the propeller defines the angle of the blades to the flow, and thus the thrust and pressure forces that are developed by the action of the blades, it is also an important feature with regard to cavitation. Because of this the pitch is usually varied over the blade surface to suit the average water speed at each radius and so to minimize the risk of cavitation.

Types of propeller

Although there are several types of propeller they all operate on the same basic principle of accelerating the water behind the ship.

The conventional propeller is a one-piece casting having two or more blades, although commonly four to six, designed specifically to operate at best efficiency at the ship's normal operating condition. Considerable effort is made to machine and finish these usually non-ferrous casting to a high degree of accuracy.

The variable pitch propeller has its blades mounted separately on the hub so that, if required, they can be swivelled by a mechanism inside the hub which is operated hydraulically from inside the ship. By changing the pitch or angle of the blades, this type of propeller can produce a variable amount of thrust to suit particular demands met in the ship's operation, such as when towing or manoeuvring. Complete control of the ship can thus be effected remotely from the bridge from full ahead to full astern without changing the direction of rotation of the engine, which would require more time.

The ducted propeller is either a conventional or controllable-pitch propeller fitted inside a 'nozzle' and because of its aerofoil shape the nozzle helps to accelerate the water flow into the propeller as well as producing a certain amount of thrust itself to propel the ship. This type of propeller has proved very efficient in special applications such as tugs and trawlers and is now being used on large bulk carriers.

Another type is the contra-rotating propeller system in which two conventional propellers are placed one in front of the other but rotating in opposite directions. The object of this is, in general, to reduce the loading per propeller, while recovering in the second propeller some of the rotational losses from the first.

Construction

Propellers are made in a variety of materials but are normally manufactured in nickle-aluminium or manganese bronzes. For a conventional propeller, a mould is first prepared using a cement-bonded sand mixture; the metal is then cast, cooled under control and finally finished to the required complex shape.

The largest solid propeller so far produced has six blades, a diameter of 31 feet (9.4 m) and weighs 72 tons: it involved the melting of about 100 tons of metal. If the size of ships increases we may yet see propellers weighing 150 tons absorbing over 80,000 horsepower.

THE RUDDER

Originally boats were manoeuvred by suspending an oar over one or both sides of the craft at the stern. Around 200 AD, the Chinese realized that a better solution lay in setting the oar vertically through a shaft in the overhanging stern deck and the rudder continued to be used in this form on Chinese junks. As a result of trade contact with the Chinese, Arab seaman began to hang the rudder like a hinged door on to the stern-post, and by the 12th century AD the rudder was in general use in the West.

Rudder action

The passage of a ship causes water to flow past the rudder, and the angle at which the rudder is inclined to the direction of flow is called the angle of attack. The steering action is dependent on the pressure distribution between the two hydrodynamic surfaces of the rudder. The pressure on the downstream side is less than the static pressure of the surrounding water, while the pressure on the upstream side is greater. The result is an outward force on the downstream side of the rudder, and this can be regarded as being made up of a lift force at right angles to the direction of flow and a drag force directly opposing the direction of flow. The variation of the lift and drag forces for different angles of attack is extremely important in rudder design as it is the lift force which creates the turning effect. At a certain angle of attack, called the critical angle, the rudder stalls: a phenomenon called burbling occurs and the rudder force is suddenly reduced. Burbling is caused by a breakdown in the streamlined flow on the downstream side of the rudder into a irregular eddying flow. Rudders on merchant vessels are normally expected to operate up to an angle of 35° from the centreline and the critical angle is important, as a reduction of rudder force would be undesirable within the working range.

Results from model tests with rudders in open water must be interpreted with care and cannot be directly applied to a ship, as the rudder action is modified by the flow of water around the hull interacting with the propeller slip. Reliable results can only be obtained from full scale ship tests, and then the model information is corrected by a suitable factor for further rudder design.

When a ship's rudder is turned, the ship first moves a small distance sideways in the opposite direction to the intended turn and then moves around a circular path until it eventually faces the opposite direction. The distance moved forward from the point at which the rudder was turned to the point at which the ship is at right angles to its original direction is called the advance. Transfer is the sideways distance between these two points, and the diameter of the circular path followed by the ship is called the tactical diameter. During the turn, the bow of the vessel lies always inside the turning curve, so that a drift angle is formed between the centreline of the vessel and the tangent to the turning curve. The tactical diameter is a measure of the ability of the rudder to turn the vessel.

Other methods of steering

A water jet unit may be used for propulsion and steering. The system is extremely useful for ferries and river craft where manoeuvring in confined waters is necessary. Water is drawn into the unit and then discharged at high speed through a set of vanes which can be rotated to give thrust in any specified direction. Two units may be fitted to a vessel, one forward and one aft, to give maximum turning effect.

A bow thrust unit consists of a water tunnel at right angles to the centre line of a ship, fitted with a propeller whose blade angle or pitch can be varied by a hydraulic control. By altering the pitch, the amount of thrust can be adjusted to give the required lateral movement of the ship. The unit is controlled from the bridge of the vessel and the propeller is driven by a motor through a flexible connection and bevel gearing. Bow thrusters are used on many ships such as oil tankers, bulk carriers and passenger vessels, and they are used for accurate course control of cable laying vessels.

A 'Navyflux' thruster, mounted in the bow of a ship, has a Y-shaped tunnel with openings at each side of the vessel and another directly forwards. An axial pump mounted in the front limb of the tunnel is used to discharge water out through the two other limbs. The openings of the two side limbs are operated by a hydraulic mechanism. A lateral force is created by arranging the shutters so that different quantities of water flow out through the two side limbs of the tunnel; the maximum steering force is obtained when one of the shutters is entirely closed, the other is fully open and the pump is operated at maximum power. This type of thruster does not require forward motion of the ship for its operation, but at high forward speeds it will operate without the pump running.

An active rudder has a propulsion unit fitted into the rudder body and a fixed or variable pitch propeller at its trailing edge. When the rudder is turned, the propeller will produce thrust at an angle to the centreline of the vessel, causing a greater turning effect than the rudder alone. Here again, the rudder is not dependent on the forward motion of the ship for its operation.

An articulated rudder has a separate flap which can be turned through a greater angle than that of the rudder. This rudder flap alters the flow characteristics of the water over the rudder by increasing the camber of the surface. For low ship speeds the articulated rudder produces a greater rudder lift force and therefore a more positive turning effect. Articulated rudders are generally fitted on fishing vessels and tugs.

A jet flap rudder has a similar action to the articulated rudder described above, but it is simpler mechanically. Water is pumped into the rudder, which is hollow, through the upper stock (the rudder turning linkage), and leaves through a vertical slot near to the trailing edge. The main jet of water emerging from this slot can be switched to the left or right by means

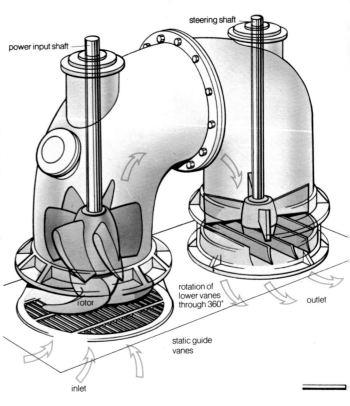

of a control chamber which is also fed with water from the upper stock. The control chamber ejects a water jet into the main jet, causing the main flow to deflect through the desired slot according to which way the vessel is to be turned.

A cycloidal propeller combines the functions of a propeller and a rudder. It has vertical blades which can be turned through specific angles to produce an overall thrust in one direction. The correct angle of each blade is set by mechanical linkages and an eccentric which controls the direction of thrust for steering purposes. One of the advantages of this system is that it allows a ship to be turned in its own length.

A cylindrical rudder consists of a vertically mounted rotatable cylinder located behind the ship's propeller. It operates by distorting the water flow around the cylinder, and this causes a lift force at right angles to the direction of fluid flow. Conventional rudders can also be fitted with rotating cylinders to modify their flow characteristics and to improve the lift force. The cylinder may be fitted at the leading edge of the rudder or just in front of a rudder flap.

The stabilizer

The ship's stabilizers are designed to reduce the rolling of the ship in rough water, in order to prevent cargo from shifting about and causing a list of the ship. Stabilizers also reduce problems for the catering services on ferries, ocean liners and cruise ships, as well as adding to passenger comfort. For accurate gunfire on warships, it is essential to keep motion as steady as possible, and stabilizers are fitted to many naval vessels to control the angle of roll. The stabilizer also reduces the stresses and strains on the ship's hull and internal framework caused by rolling. Various types of stabilizer have been tried with varying degrees of success; these include bilge keels, oscillating weights, anti-rolling tanks, gyroscopes and stabilizer fins.

Bilge keels

These are normally fitted to the hull along both sides of the ship, and they extend for about one-third of the length of the vessel. They are riveted or welded to the shell where it curves to form the bilge at the bottom of the ship. Bilge keels are attached so that they offer minimum resistance to the forward motion, and they are not too strongly connected to the hull so that they will break off without damaging the shell if they strike an obstruction. They present resistance to motion in the rolling direction by impeding the fluid flow around the hull, and they are more effective when the ship is under way than when it is stationery. Bilge keels are fairly effective at damping out the angle of roll, and they tend to increase the period of roll, that is the time taken to roll from one side to the other and back again.

Oscillating weights

This system, now out of favour, involves moving weights from one side of a vessel to the other to counteract the motion created by the sea. The phase of

In the jet propulsion unit (above) water is forced through the U-shaped tunnel and the outlet vanes deflect the water in the direction desired.
The Kamewa bow thrust unit (centre) has a propeller in a tunnel at a right angle to the line of the ship; the propeller can drive water in either direction by altering the pitch of the blades. The Navy flux thruster (below) drives water out on either side of the ship by opening the appropriate shutters. The jet flap rudder drives water through a port or starboard aperture (lower right).

controllable pitch propeller

Navyflux Y-thruster in the bulbous bow of a vessel

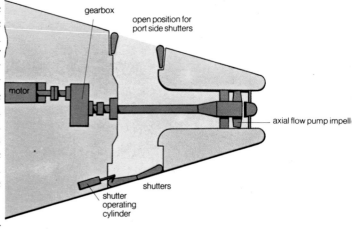

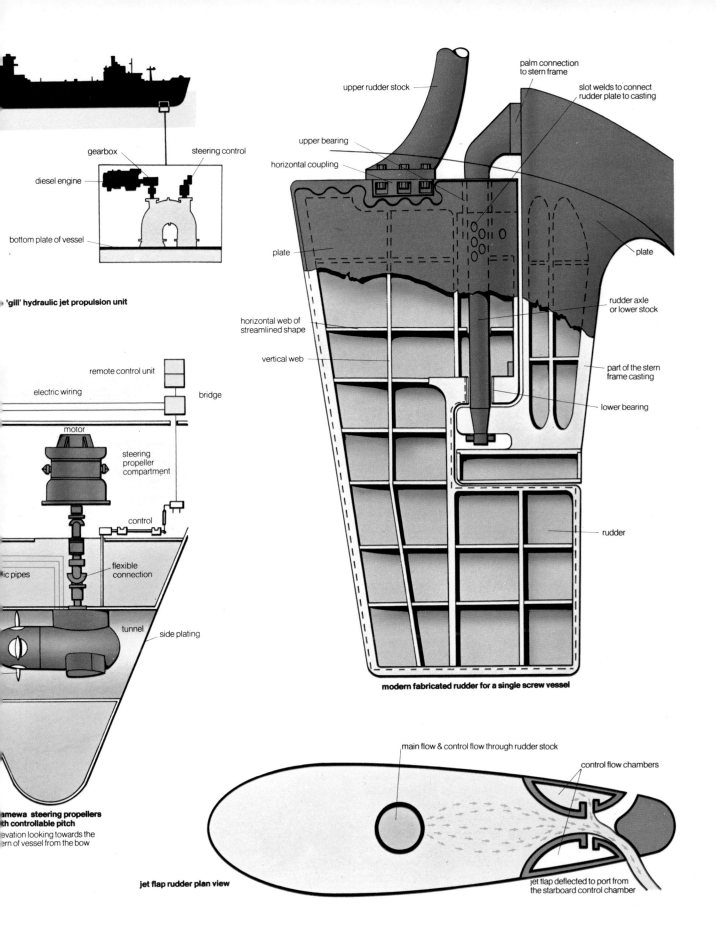

gearbox

steering control

diesel engine

bottom plate of vessel

'gill' hydraulic jet propulsion unit

remote control unit

electric wiring

bridge

motor

steering propeller compartment

control

flexible connection

...ic pipes

tunnel

side plating

...amewa steering propellers
...th controllable pitch
...evation looking towards the
...ern of vessel from the bow

upper rudder stock

palm connection to stern frame

slot welds to connect rudder plate to casting

upper bearing

horizontal coupling

plate

plate

horizontal web of streamlined shape

vertical web

rudder axle or lower stock

part of the stern frame casting

lower bearing

rudder

modern fabricated rudder for a single screw vessel

main flow & control flow through rudder stock

control flow chambers

jet flap rudder plan view

jet flap deflected to port from the starboard control chamber

*Right: a stabilizer fin
mounted on a ship's hull.
It counteracts the rolling
motion of the ship
according to its angle of
attack.*

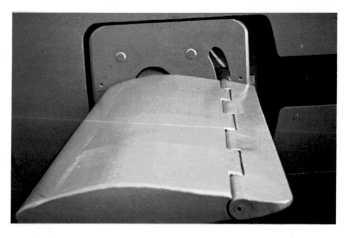

the weight movement must lag 90 degrees behind the rolling motion of the vessel (the two movements must always be out of step) and thus the timing of the operation is critical. One method tried in an experimental installation was to move a truck on curved rails so that its weight produced a stabilizing force on the ship. Systems of this sort are no longer used partly because control in irregular waves is difficult and partly because they are noisy.

Anti-rolling tanks

These were introduced very shortly after the first use of bilge keels. 'Frahm' anti-rolling tanks have been successfully used for a number of years on many ships. They are usually fitted near to amidships, either in a tween deck space or lower down in the vessel above the double bottom. The arrangement is like a U-tube but with a larger cross-sectional area in the two vertical legs than in the horizontal leg. The relationship between these areas is important because the period of fluid oscillation when the ship rolls must be similar, but 90 degrees out of phase to that of the ship. There must be an air connection between the tops of the vertical tanks; otherwise the air in one tank will become pressurized and the other tank will have a partial vacuum when the liquid levels change. An air valve in the connection gives a means of fluid control if necessary.

In activated anti-rolling tanks a high capacity, low pressure air compressor supplies air to the upper part of the tanks, and by varying the pressure in each tank water can be moved from one side of the ship to the other to give a stabilizing effect. A gyroscope is used to stop and start the compressor and to operate the tank air valves as it senses the ship's motion.

Gyroscopic stabilizers

Some vessels are fitted with large gyroscopes to control rolling. This technique reduces the average angle of roll by about 50%. Schlick in Germany was the first to use this system, and later Sperry stabilizers were introduced in the United States. The Schlick gyroscope was installed with the spin axis vertical, and the support frame axis horizontal. When the vessel rolls the gyroscope frame swings in its bearings in a fore and aft direction. This is called precession and is a function of the gyroscopic action. A roll to starboard would cause the top of the gyroscope frame to move aft if unresisted at the bearings. The opposite will occur for a roll to port. Because the rolling of the ship causes precession of the gyroscope, if precessional motion is resisted by applying brakes to the bearings of the support frame this will set up a stabilizing effect in opposition to the rolling of the ship. Brake control of the Schlick type of stabilizer is difficult to achieve, and the Sperry stabilizers were arranged with a precession motor meshed with a vertical ring gear to precess the gyroscope in a direction to oppose the rolling motion of the ship. Control of the precession motor is by a small pilot gyroscope sensitive to the transverse motion of the ship.

The pilot gyroscope operates electrical contacts which power the precession motor in the required direction.

Flume stabilization

A flume tank is placed transversely across the ship and comprises two side compartments and a centre compartment, which contain water. The motion of the fluid from one side of the vessel to the other is controlled by a restriction called a flume. Liquid depth is constant in the centre compartment during the transfer process. The tanks are carefully designed to tune the liquid frequency to the natural period of roll of the vessel and to maintain the 90 degree phase relationship necessary for stabilization. The flume prevents the liquid movement from coming into phase with the ship's movement and causing a disastrous increase in the rolling.

Fins

Stabilizer fins project from the hull and produce a turning movement on the ship to oppose any rolling motion. As the ship moves through the water, the flow over the protruding fins, port and starboard, is deflected according to the angle of the fin, producing either an upward or a downward force. As the ship rolls, the fin on the ascending side of the vessel will generate a downward force and the fin on the other side will produce an upward force. The magnitude of these forces depends on the angle through which the fins are rotated from the horizontal position, and the speed of the water over the fin surface. The fins are moved by an oil operated vane motor which receives its supply from a gyroscopically controlled hydraulic pump. At low ship speeds the fins are not so effective as when the vessel is travelling at her designed cruising speed. When not in use the fins may be retracted into a watertight box in the hull.

ANTI-FOULING TECHNIQUES

Anti-fouling techniques are used to keep ships' hulls and other objects which are submerged in the sea, such as buoys and oil rigs, free from animals and vegetation. Unchecked infestation will severely decrease the speed of a ship and will require additional fuel to overcome the drop in performance. To this must be added the cost of docking, loss of earnings and the financial burden of carrying out remedial measures.

The organisms which settle on ships' hulls disturb the smooth flow of water and cause an increase in drag which turns out in practice to be 0.25% per day for temperate waters. After six months, a ship's top speed may be cut by up to 2 knots, and about 40% more fuel is used in keeping up cruising speed. The most common fouling species are barnacles and green algae, but in some regions tube-worms, hydroids, sea-squirts, mussels, and various red and brown algae also give trouble. Even when killed, barnacles cause an increase in drag by the presence of their empty shells.

Anti-fouling paints are still the most efficient means of achieving protection. They contain toxicants, chemicals that are poisonous to fouling organisms. Cuprous oxide is the most universally used but it is often 'boosted' with other compounds such as tributyltin oxide. In order to be effective, the toxicants have to dissolve out of the paint into the surrounding water.

Types of coating

There are two types of anti-fouling paints, the first in which the matrix (base material) is insoluble and the second in which it is slightly soluble. Included in the former are materials such as vinyls, and in the latter the acidic resin known as rosin.

Soluble matrix coatings, being slightly acidic, react with the seawater, thus slowly releasing the toxicant.

With paints of the insoluble kind new layers of cuprous oxide particles are exposed to the seawater as the outer ones dissolve, while the matrix itself remains in place. In addition there are coatings which rely on mechanical erosion, produced by the water flow over the surface, to expose the toxicant which then dissolves in the water.

Ancient practice

The fouling problem is a very ancient one. As early as 200 BC the Greek writer Atheneus records that the ships of Archimedes were fastened with copper bolts and the entire bottom sheathed with lead. The first consideration in those days was to prevent the wood-destroying 'ship-worm' and 'gribble' from attacking the timbers, although the benefits of controlling fouling were realized.

In the 4th and 5th centuries the Phoenicians, Carthaginians and Greeks used a variety of methods which included coatings of pitch, wax and a mixture of arsenic, sulphur and oil. Such practices were continued for centuries, but provided only short-term protection.

The Phoenicians are also said to have employed copper sheathing, but it was not until the 18th century that this material was widely used. The first authenticated case was that of the Royal Naval vessel, HMS *Alarm*, in 1759. The absence of fouling was noted but the cause remained a mystery. It was not until 1824, as result of the researches of Sir Humphrey Davy, that the toxic effects of dissolved copper were recognised.

The disadvantages of using copper sheathing were

Below: the effect of anti-fouling on steel. The section on the right was not treated; algae and barnacles have collected. At left is only a mud slime. The red colour is the cuprous oxide.

THE ANCHOR

that it was expensive and it dissolved comparatively rapidly, causing the iron nails used in the construction of the ship and the rudder irons to corrode.

With the evolution of iron and steel hulled ships, the corrosive electrolytic reaction between copper and the metal of the hull, made the use of such sheathing totally impractical. It was then that the scientists turned their attention to developing anti-fouling coatings.

Traditionally, it was considered that the average time between dry-dockings for defouling was six to nine months. Present day anti-fouling paints can give protection for two and a half to three years.

It has been calculated that the war against Japan was shortened by as much as 18 months because Japanese anti-fouling techniques lagged behind those of the United States. The enemy ships had to return to port for defouling every nine months and it was supposed that American ships would have to do the same. On several occasions the Japanese attacked targets expecting US guard ships to be safely in dry dock when in fact they were not, and as a consequence the attacker sustained heavy losses.

At present, attention is being paid to developing improved anti-fouling paints, more effective toxicants, alternative methods of distributing these compounds, and methods which do not require the use of toxicants at all. In the latter case, research is trying to find compounds, both synthetic and natural, which do not kill organisms but make it impossible for them to attach themselves to the craft.

An anchor moors a vessel to the sea bed, generally by a combination of its own weight and by hooking itself into the bottom. A typical anchor is shaped so that a horizontal pull causes it to dig itself in firmly, but an upward pull dislodges it easily. It is attached to the vessel by a cable or, in the case of large ships, a heavy chain. The cable must lie flat for some distance along the sea bed if the anchor is to be effective, and the length of cable needed for this is from three to eight times the depth of water.

Unmooring, or 'weighing' the anchor, is carried out by winching in the cable. This pulls the vessel over the anchor's position, and when the cable is more or less vertical the anchor should dislodge.

The earliest anchors were simple stone weights: the mud-weight is still used on inland waterways for cruising craft. Underwater archaeologists have found a large number of stone anchors of different shapes and sizes in the Mediterranean, some dating back at least to the Bronze Age. One of the most common types was a roughly triangular stone with a hole in the top corner for the cable. Sometimes there were holes in the bottom corners, perhaps for wooden flukes or digging ends. Some time after 1000 BC metal began to be used, with huge wooden anchors with lead stocks (crosspieces). Around this time the traditional fixed anchor evolved which was used well into the 19th century.

The flukes of this type of anchor are on arms which are set at right angles to the top crosspiece, or stock. If, when an anchor first touches the sea bottom, the stock is the first part to dig in, the anchor will tend to twist

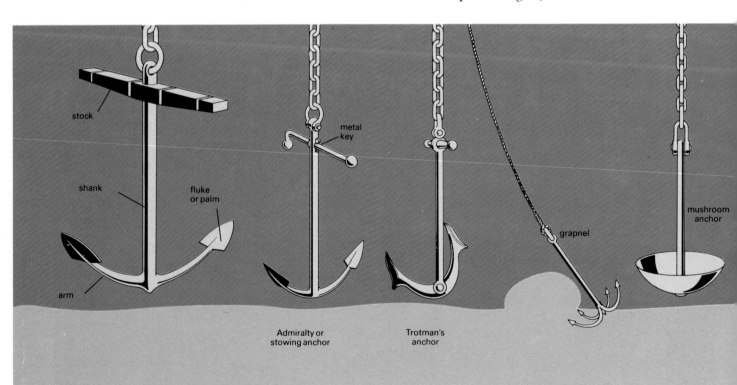

stock

shank

fluke or palm

arm

metal key

Admiralty or stowing anchor

Trotman's anchor

grapnel

mushroom anchor

over when pulled so that a fluke is stuck in instead.

Large anchors of this type were rather unwieldy on board ship, so the stowing type was invented, which has a stock with one bent end. It is held in place by a metal key when being used, but can be folded flat along the length of the anchor for stowing. This type, sometimes called the Admiralty anchor, is commonly found in yachts and other small craft.

The effectiveness of a type of anchor depends on the nature of the sea bed. The Admiralty anchor does not hold well on a soft bottom, since the digging area is fairly small. A variation which helped to overcome this is the Trotman's anchor, which has its flukes on pivoted arms to allow them to dig in at the most effective angle.

The anchor used on most large modern ships is the stockless anchor. The large flukes of this type are pivoted, and can move out from the anchor by a maximum of 45°. Projections on the flukes called tripping palms make sure that the flukes stick into the sea bed. A horizontal pull on the cable makes them dig in even more. As the device has no stock, it can be pulled up to the mouth of the hawse pipe until only the arms and flukes are protruding, so it is always ready for use.

One variation of this is the Danforth, which uses a small stock at the bottom of the anchor to stabilize it. Another, the CQR or plough anchor, has a single fluke shaped like a ploughshare, which digs itself deeper as more pull is applied.

Other forms of anchor include the grapnel, with four or five arms to snag in projections on the sea bed, which can also be used to drag for lost objects. The mushroom anchor has a shape which is ideal for permanently mooring lightships and dredgers to a soft sea bed. Its mushroom shape tends to sink deeply and hold in place by suction, though because this takes some time to happen a straightforward weight is often used for the purpose.

The sea anchor is a structure of wood and canvas shaped rather like a large sock. It is paid out over the bows of a vessel, and the drag brings the craft round so that it faces the direction of the oncoming waves. This is useful when a vessel is not under way in a heavy sea, for example. Small vessels may use similar devices, called drogues, from the stern to steady them when sailing with the wind in a heavy sea. In an emergency, a plastic bucket serves the same purpose.

Below: a sequence of drawings of types of anchors which have been used. Another variation is the rond, which has only one fluke and no stock and is simply stuck in the bank by hand. At the far right is the stockless anchor, which has tripping palms on it. When a palm is dragged along the sea bed it helps the fluke turn into the bottom.

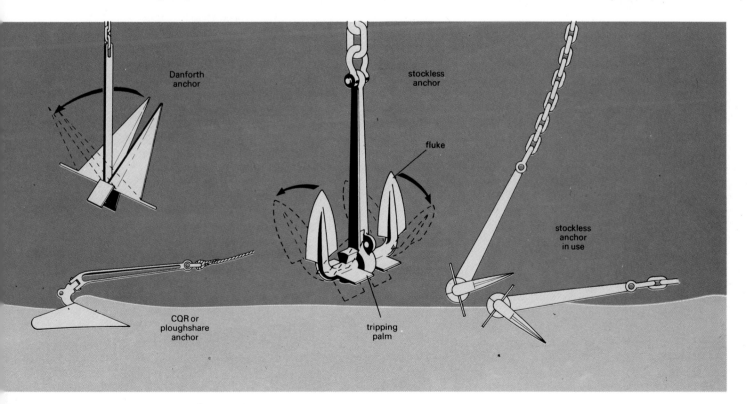

THE ASTROLABE

The astrolabe is an ancient astronomical instrument which had a wide variety of uses concerned with measuring and predicting the positions of the sun and stars. The word literally means 'star-taker'.

The earliest and basic type is called the *planispheric* astrolabe. It was probably invented by the Greeks or Alexandrians about 100 BC or even earlier, and was later developed by the Arabs.

In principle it is a simple model, or analogue, of the Earth and sky, reduced to two flat discs. These are usually made of brass, and are up to 10 inches (25 cm) across. One of these, the plate, represents the Earth and is marked with lines of latitude, longitude, the observer's horizon and other lines indicating angles above the horizon. It has to be designed for use at a particular latitude, so it was common for several plates to be

THE SEXTANT

provided, giving a range of useful latitudes.

The other disc is called the *rete* (Latin for net) or *spider* because of its appearance: it is a simple map of the sky with the positions of bright stars shown by curved pointers. The line of the ecliptic—the zodiac, or Sun's path among the stars — is also shown.

These two discs are mounted on another called the mater which has a scale of hours around the outside. The rete is free to rotate about the centre.

This device can be set to show the appearance of the sky for any date and time. In order to measure the actual positions of the Sun and stars, a sighting device called an *alidade* is mounted on the same spindle but on the back of the mater, which has a degree scale marked around its outer edge. The astrolabe is suspended by a ring at the top, to give the vertical. The alidade could also be used for surveying, to find the height of a building for example. In this case, a rectangular scale was used, with a horizontal arm representing ground level and an upright arm representing the building. The observer stood at the edge of the building's shadow and hung the astrolabe so that the shadow of one end of the alidade fell on the other end. Then the angles on the back of the astrolabe were the same as those of the building and shadow, and the height of the building could be calculated.

Before astronomical almanacs or tables became common, the astrolabe was used to find the time of day, the rising and setting times of the Sun and stars, the direction of Mecca, and so on. To peoples far more dependent on the Sun, stars and astrology than we are, the astrolabe was invaluable. When astronomical calculations became more accurate and mechanical clocks more reliable the astrolabe became unnecessary, though its use continued in Arab countries into the 19th century.

The astrolabe was very widely used in western Europe in the 14th century—Geoffrey Chaucer wrote a well known *Treatise on the Astrolabe* in 1391—and even after it became obsolete in the 17th century it was still a fashionable ornament.

The mariner's astrolabe was developed chiefly by the Portuguese in the 15th century as an observing instrument pure and simple. It was used to measure the height above the horizon of the Sun or a star at sea, so that the latitude could be found. It dispensed with the plate and rete and was heavy enough to hang vertically despite a ship's movement. With the invention of the quadrant, the forerunner of the sextant, in the 17th century, it went out of use.

A form of astrolabe can still be bought quite cheaply, though the intricate and beautiful classical instruments are now rare. The modern version, made of plastic, is called a planisphere and can be set to show the appearance of the night sky at any time during the year.

Left: this astrolabe was made in 1572. The curved pointers indicate stars, not always bright ones; the scales underneath are for use in the tropics.

Astrolabes and quadrants were variations on the theme of a sighting bar moved along a scale of degrees. In most cases it was necessary to view both the star and the horizon at the same time from the deck of the ship, and it is not surprising that the observations were inaccurate. In the case of the quadrant the reference point was not the horizon but a plumb line attached to the scale. This made it possible to concentrate on the star only, but the plumb line could easily swing about, leading to further errors.

The device which replaced these, the forerunner of the sextant, was the octant, invented by James Hadley in 1731. The principle and design of the octant was nearly the same as that of any sextant in daily use nowadays: the main difference is that the octant had a scale which was one eighth of a circle, 45°, while a sextant has a scale of one sixth of a circle, 60°. Because both devices measure an angle which is reflected by a mirror, the octant will measure angles up to 90° and the sextant angles up to 120°. The octant was often referred to as a quadrant because it had the same range as one, though its scale was only 45°. In practice, few sextants measure 120°, but the name is retained.

Hadley's invention was to use a pair of small mirrors to reflect the image of the star to be observed so that it appeared to be on the horizon. The navigator could keep both in view at the same time, and as the ship rolled both would move together. The movable mirror was attached to the pivot of the movable index bar, at the radius of the scale or arc, so that as the angle was changed so the mirror would move. This mirror reflected the star's image to a second mirror, permanently set to view the first one. The navigator looked through a sight to the second mirror, past which he could see the horizon. He moved the first by moving the index bar until the star's image reflected by both mirrors exactly touched the horizon. The angle was then read off the arc, which was graduated in degrees (but twice as closely as a true scale of degrees, to allow for the mirror's reflection).

Hadley's octant was immediately accepted by navigators. In 1757, John Campbell introduced the true sextant which was capable of measuring a greater angle. Captain Cook was probably the first to fully apply the potential of the sextant for measuring not only vertical angles but also angles at any inclination. By measuring the angle between the Moon and a given star, he could calculate the precise time, using tables of the Moon's motion, enabling him to find his longitude as well as the latitude—the method used for the charting of New Zealand during the voyage of 1768-1771. The invention of accurate timekeepers made the procedure unnecessary, and the sextant was then used to measure the altitude of stars or the Sun at precise times, thus giving the longitude whenever required.

Although the earliest sextants and octants had simple sighting devices, the accuracy was much improved by the use of a small telescope. The second mirror, the horizon mirror, would only be silvered across half its width so that the telescope would show both the horizon and the star side by side. Dark filters could be moved into the light paths to cut down the brightness of the Sun or horizon.

The sextant has remained basically unchanged from 1800 to the present day, but there have been some changes to the way in which the arm of the sextant is made to travel along the arc. In the early days there was no fine adjustment screw and the navigator merely moved the arm along the arc and clamped it to the frame so that the reading could be taken. On a moving

deck this could be a difficult operation and in the 1760s a fine adjustment tangent screw was added. This meant that the operator could quickly take his sight to the nearest degree and then, by using the tangent screw, make the final close adjustment. The only drawback with the clamping variety of sextant was that the tangent screw frequently had to be returned to its starting position, otherwise it would come to the limit of its thread as a sighting was being taken. The problem was solved in the 1920s. A toothed rack was cut into the sextant frame and the tangent screw was now meshed into this. The arm could be moved along the arc by pressing a quick release catch, and the tangent screw could travel the full length of the arc without being reset.

The sextants of this period were still using the finely engraved scale, which had to be read with a magnifier, as they had been over the previous hundred years. Around 1933 the modern micrometer sextant was evolved. Instead of engraving the fine divisions on the arc, they were transferred to an enlarged tangent screw head, thereby doing away with the magnifier and making the sextant easier to read.

Other types
The sextant may still be used for air navigation far from the busy air corridors. In this case the horizon cannot be used as it is below the true horizontal, and a system which reflects the image of a bubble level into the field of view is used. Astrodomes, small transparent domes into which the sextant will fit, may be set into the top of the aircraft, or in the case of the faster aircraft a periscope system will be fitted.

Above: older sextants had clamps to stop the arm of the bar, which could be adjusted by a screw thread; the modern instrument simply has a vernier screw gauge. Modern optics has shortened the telescope.
Right: sextant procedure is to adjust the index mirror until the edge of the Sun just touches the horizon. The reading is corrected to give the centre of the Sun.

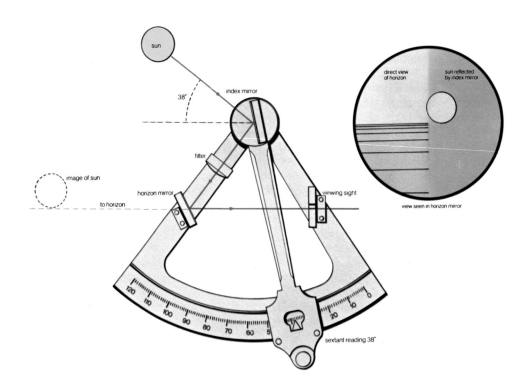

THE COMPASS

The observation that the iron mineral called lodestone would align itself in a northerly direction was recorded in China in the first century BC. There is little evidence that this discovery resulted in the development of a floating compass until about AD 1100. By about AD 1250 the compass was being used by the Arabs, Scandinavians and Europeans as well as the Chinese. When European explorers first penetrated Chinese waters, they found the Chinese compass much inferior to their own. It is impossible to say where the development of the compass first took place, or whether it developed independently in the East and the West.

Early development

By the thirteenth century magnetized iron 'needles were used as compasses floated or pivoted in conjunction with a scale (the wind-rose) showing the direction of the prevailing Mediterranean winds, to indicate north when the sky was cloudy. Later the scales, or cards, were marked with the four cardinal points, north, south, east and west, and further subdivided to give a total of 32 points. Subsequently a scale of degrees was made: 0° at N and S; 90° at E and W, making a total of 360°. (The arbitrary number of 360 degrees in a circle is an inheritance from ancient Babylonian astronomers. When measuring time, they had divided the day into six parts which were further subdivided by six. These measurements were originally land distance measurements, which were extended to cover the sky, making a circle. This division of the circle also survives in the time measurements of modern astronomy.)

During the fifteenth century it was discovered that there was a slight difference in the compass reading between true north (the direction of the North Pole) and magnetic north. The angle of the difference is called magnetic declination, or variation and it can now be determined for a particular locality from charts. On his second voyage, in 1493, Columbus carried compasses which had been altered in an attempt to allow for variation. The great geographer and map-maker Gerhardus Mercator (1512-1594) was the first to correctly assume the existence of a magnetic pole separate from the North Pole. William Gilbert (1544-1603), in his *De Magnete* (1600), was the first to propose that the Earth itself was a great magnet, but he thought variation was caused by the magnetic attraction of land masses. The first modern charts giving world variations were published in 1701 by Edmond Halley (1656-1742), of comet fame.

Mariner's direct-reading compass

The iron needle originally used in compasses needed frequent remagnetization. In 1766 Dr G Knight patented a compass in England which was the most advanced design of its time. He used a better magnet steel for the needle, a jewelled bearing for the pivot to minimize friction and wear, and suspended the compass on pivots inside a ring (the gimbal) to provide insulation from the ship's motion.

Further improvements were made by mounting the compass in a liquid-filled bowl, thus damping it from mechanical vibrations. This was complicated on the earliest models by such factors as the leakage or bursting of the bowl due to atmospheric conditions, and the discoloration or corrosion of the compass parts because of impurities in the damping liquid.

In the meantime other improvements were made to the mounting stand of the compass (the binnacle). During the nineteenth century, as shipbuilders began to use more iron in construction, ships were lost on account of magnetic interference with the ship's compass. The solution to the problem, proposed by Britain's Admiralty Compass Committee, was to install in the binnacle a system of compensation for 'hard' and 'soft' iron respectively by separate assembles of magnets and masses of soft iron. 'Hard' iron refers to the iron in the ship's structure and 'soft' iron to changes in the direction of the ship's magnetic field with respect

Above: an azimuth compass with sights, made in London about 1770. It would have been used for taking bearings.

87

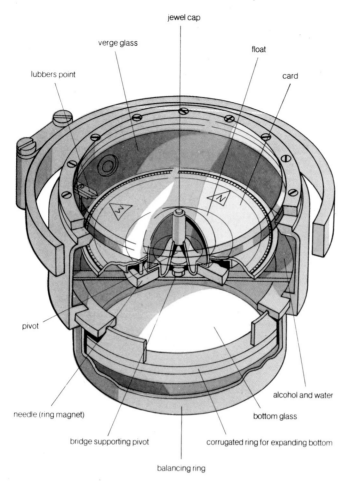

jewel cap
verge glass
float
lubbers point
card
needle (ring magnet)
pivot
alcohol and water
bottom glass
bridge supporting pivot
corrugated ring for expanding bottom
balancing ring

Left: the float pivots in a liquid bath, the card is attached to the float and the magnet suspended from the card.

field around the ship's hull in order to prevent setting off magnetic mines. This necessitates an electric compensating device at the binnacle of the ship's compass.

Remote-indicating compasses

These are compasses which electrically relay their reading to remotely located dials. Radar installations, missile tracking devices and other such equipment may have the compass remotely located because of electromagnetic interference with the magnet.

A remote-indicating compass may take the form of a magnetometer assembly which measures components of the Earth's magnetic field relative to the vehicle axis and, after suitable processing, passes the information electrically to conveniently sited indicators. In aircraft the detector unit will be situated in a magnetically 'clean' place such as the wingtip or tail assembly. Typically the magnetometer consists of a core, which is magnetized by the Earth's field, carrying windings; a current is passed through these windings to counteract the Earth's field. Sometimes a conventional magnetic compass is adapted so that the orientation of its system can be detected using bridge circuits connected to electrodes which are located on the pointer and card, or photo-electric cells which pick up a beam of light passing through a hole in the card. Subsidiary magnetometers may also be used, the electrical signal being used again for transmission.

Other compass designs

The gyromagnetic compass is a compass mounted on a stable base which is always kept horizontal by an electrically operated gyroscope, no matter what the attitude of the vehicle. This was developed for submarines, aircraft and small boats whose acceleration might cause a compass needle to be affected by a vertical field. The gyromagnetic compass should not be confused with the gyrocompass, which does not use magnetism.

Gyrocompass

The gyrocompass is a true north directional indicator used extensively in merchant and naval vessels. It is one of the most useful navigation aids, as it provides a true north indication regardless of any rolling, pitching or yawing of the vessel and is entirely unaffected by any of the disturbances which commonly affect magnetic compasses. The gyrocompass is usually installed below deck and its indication is relayed around the ship to operate ancillary equipment such as steering and bearing repeaters, course recorders and gyropilots.

The basis of the gyrocompass is a gyroscope controlled in such a way that its spin axis is made to seek and maintain alignment with the geographic meridian (north-south line). This is achieved by combining the characteristics of the gyroscope, inertia and precession, with natural phenomena, the Earth's rotation and the force of gravity.

Theory of operation

The Earth rotates about its polar axis from west to east with an angular velocity of one revolution in 24

to that of the Earth. (Random magnetic interference is minimized by placing offending objects a pre-determined safe distance away from the binnacle.) A ship's magnetic field is determined by trial and error experiments, but once the adjustments are made the compass should only need checking once a year. If a ship is struck by lightning or heavily damaged in military operations, the magnetic field will go awry and may take months to settle down.

The modern mariner's compass

A typical 'standard' compass has a 360° card six to nine inches (15 to 22.5 cm) in diameter supported by a jewelled bearing on an osmium-iridium or tungsten carbide pivot in a liquid filled bowl, it carries either a pair of bar magnets or a single 'ring' magnet with its poles along a diameter. The reference mark, or lubber, is a pointer protruding to the edge of the card from the inner wall of the bowl. A float enables the system to be adjusted to about $\frac{1}{4}$ oz (7 g) minimizing wear and prolonging pivot life. The liquid is commonly an alcohol and water mixture or a light oil. Apart from the system magnet all materials must be strictly non-magnetic. The compass bowl is suspended through gimbal rings at the top of the binnacle, which carries lighting and means for compensating for the unwanted fields created by the ship. Means are also provided for mounting a prism, an azimuth circle or other device for taking bearings on top of the compass bowl.

On some ships, in order to isolate the compass bowl more fully from the ship's magnetic field the compass is mounted overhead, and the card illuminated from behind. On some military vessels since World War II provision has been made for setting up a neutralizing

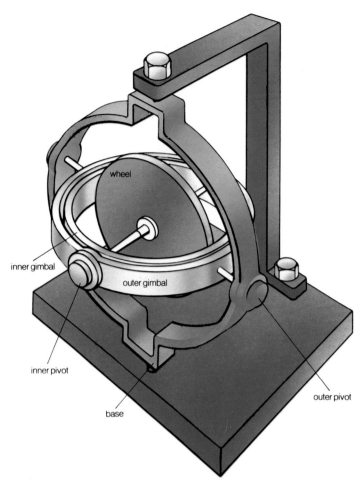

Right: a gyroscope with gimbal rings, showing how the rotor has freedom to maintain any given position.

wheel

inner gimbal

outer gimbal

inner pivot

outer pivot

base

hours, that is, 15°/h. At any point on the Earth's surface this angular velocity can be resolved into two components: a component aligned to the local vertical, known as the vertical earth rate, and a horizontal component aligned to the meridian and known as the horizontal earth rate.

The magnitude of these components varies with latitude. Vertical earth rate varies as the sine of the angle of latitude and is 15°/h at the poles and zero at the equator, while the horizontal earth rate varies as the cosine of the angle of latitude and is zero at the poles and 15°/h at the equator.

The gyroscope used in the gyrocompass is electrically driven and mounted in gimbals in such a way that it has freedom to move about both a vertical and a horizontal axis. The gyroscope can be considered as a space stable element because its axes will remain pointed in the same direction with respect to inertial space unless acted upon by a force. The Earth is not a part of inertial space but rotates within it, and so the directions in which the axes of a gyroscope point, with respect to an observer on Earth, will appear to change as the Earth rotates although they are in fact remaining constant with respect to inertial space.

Being a space stable element, the gyroscope 'senses' the rotation of the Earth: the vertical axis senses the vertical earth rate and the horizontal axis the horizontal earth rate. For this reason the effect of the Earth's rotation on the axes of the gyroscope varies with the latitude. This can best be appreciated by considering the behaviour of the gyroscope at various geographical locations.

If the gyro is located at the North Pole with its spin axis horizontal, the rotation of the Earth will be measured entirely by the vertical axis, and to an observer using the spinning Earth as a reference the space stable gyro appears to drift about its vertical axis at Earth rate, 15°/h.

When the gyro is mounted at the equator with its spin axis pointing east to west its horizontal axis is aligned with the meridian (the direction of horizontal Earth rate). and to an observer standing on the Earth the space stable gyro appears to rotate about its horizontal axis at Earth rate. This effect is referred to as 'tilting'.

With the gyro still mounted at the equator but with its spin axis pointing north to south, the tilting effect due to the rotation of the Earth is zero since the sensitive horizontal axis is displaced by 90° from the meridian. With the spin axis pointing in an intermediate position, the horizontal Earth rate affects the horizontal axis by an amount proportional to the displacement of the spin axis from the meridian.

Practical gyrocompasses

It is the effect of horizontal Earth rate that makes it possible to apply the force of gravity to convert the space stable gyroscope into a north seeking gyrocompass. When the gyro spin axis is aligned to the meridian there is no tilting effect about the horizontal axis. When

the spin axis is east of meridian, horizontal Earth rate causes the north end of the gyro to fall. The rate of tilt of the gyro is directly related to the value of the horizontal Earth rate (15°/h cosine latitude) and the misalignment of the spin axis from the meridian.

At points between the poles and the equator, the gyro appears to turn partly about its horizontal axis and partly about its vertical axis because it is affected by both horizontal and vertical earth rates. In general the horizontal Earth rate causes the gyro to tilt and the vertical earth rate causes it to rotate in azimuth (horizontally) with respect to the meridians.

A gravity reference system is used to measure any tilting of the gyro and produce torques (turning forces) to precess the gyro spin axis into alignment with the meridian. Early gyrocompasses used a weight to sense tilt and provide a north seeking force; the weight, being secured to the bottom of the gyro case, forced the spin axis to remain level as a result of its reaction with gravity and the resulting torque precessed the gyro towards the north. The principle was used by Dr. Elmer Sperry on his early gyrocompasses, one of which was successfully demonstrated aboard the USS *Delaware* in 1911 and is now on view at the Smithsonian Institution in Washington DC.

By the early 1920s this weight arrangement had been replaced by a 'ballistic' comprising two containers half filled with fluid, mounted on the north and south ends of the gyro, and interconnected by two small diameter tubes. Any tilting of the gyro caused displacement of fluid from the higher to the lower container and the resulting imbalance precessed the gyro towards the meridian. While improved versions of this system are still widely used today, electrical devices are now extensively used in gyrocompass gravity reference systems because of their great flexibility. Such systems employ accelerometers and other devices to detect tilt and the output of the device is amplified to drive the gyro torque motors.

As already mentioned, it is the relatively slow rotation of the Earth that provides the motive power for the north seeking precessional movement of the gyro-compass. When a vessel is travelling over the Earth's surface, however, and therefore about the Earth's centre, the vessel's movement is compounded with that of the Earth and will impair the accuracy of the gyro-compass. Compensation systems have been designed to counteract these errors and leave the gyro accurately aligned to the geographic north.

Astrocompass

In certain circumstances, conventional methods of direction finding can break down. Close to the Earth's poles, for example, magnetic and gyrocompasses become unreliable. The force on a magnetic needle becomes nearly vertical, and the stability of the gyro-compass becomes affected by the rotation of the Earth. Magnetic compasses can also give false readings on board metal vehicles or craft. When this happens, the most reliable direction information comes from the Sun, moon, stars and planets. Devices that use astro-nomical bodies to show compass directions are called astrocompasses.

The Earth's pole always points in the same direction in space, whatever the time of year. So for any point on the Earth's surface, the same stars will always follow the same paths through the sky. Their exact position depends on the time and geographical location at which they are observed.

The principle of the astrocompass is to calculate, from a knowledge of the time and observing site, where a particular astronomical object ought to be, and to set the instrument's sights accordingly. The device is then turned until the object is actually seen in the sights. If everything else has been set correctly, the instrument is now aligned north-south.

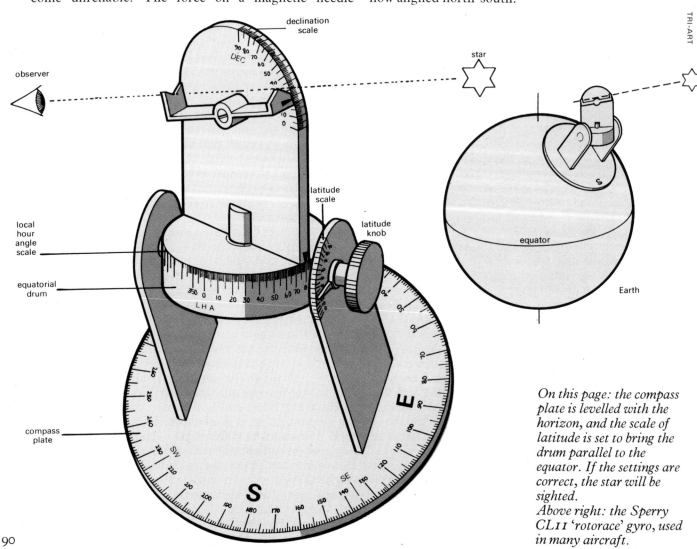

TRI-ART

On this page: the compass plate is levelled with the horizon, and the scale of latitude is set to bring the drum parallel to the equator. If the settings are correct, the star will be sighted.
Above right: the Sperry CL11 'rotorace' gyro, used in many aircraft.

ASDIC AND SONAR

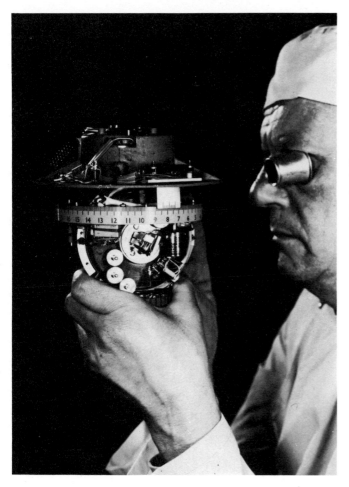

In practice, a scale marked with the points of the compass is levelled and rotated until it is believed to be roughly north-south. Mounted on this is the equatorial drum which can be tilted in this north-south direction and thus set to the latitude of the location. This means that the drum is then parallel with the equator. On the drum is a scale of Local Hour Angle, which is the angle in the sky as seen by the observer which corresponds to longitude on Earth. Longitude is measured east or west from Greenwich, while Local Hour Angle is measured east from the observer. At noon local time at any place, the Sun's Local Hour Angle is 0°; at other times, it can be found for any astronomical body using tables in the *Nautical Almanac* and a knowledge of the time and longitude at the place of observation.

Mounted on the drum is a scale of declination which is the angle of an astronomical object north or south of the equator—the celestial equivalent of latitude. A pair of sights are set to indicate the known declination of the object being used.

Having adjusted the latitude, Local Hour Angle and declination scales, the object should now be in the sights. If not, the compass is turned until it is, and the scale on the base will then show the true points of the compass.

Astrocompasses were used as checks on more conventional compasses, particularly during the Second World War in the North African Desert. Sun compasses were designed for use during the day, and some varieties had a clock mechanism incorporated so that the value of the Local Hour Angle was automatically provided. The development of electronic navigational aids has made the astrocompass obsolete.

Asdic (called after the Allied Submarine Detection Investigation Committee) is a device developed originally for detecting submarines by means of sound waves travelling through water. Its usefulness has now been extended to include detecting submerged wrecks and shoals of fish, as a navigational aid for ships, measuring the depth of water under a ship, and for research purposes. Sonar stands for sound navigation ranging and this name has largely replaced the name Asdic.

Another term, 'echo sounding', implies the principle of the system. Sound is normally thought of as being air vibrations, but water can also transmit vibrations. By listening for echoes, a picture of the area below the surface can be obtained.

In the basic technique, a short pulse of sound, which may be within the range audible to humans or may be on a much higher frequency, is transmitted from the bottom of the ship, usually by way of a transducer mounted in a hole cut in the ship's bottom. (A transducer is any device that converts electrical power into another form, such as sound, or vice versa). The sound pulse travels downwards until it strikes the sea bottom or a submerged object, which reflects it back to the ship. There, it is picked up by another transducer, and the time taken for the pulse to travel down and back is measured. The speed at which sound travels in water depends on temperature, but it is roughly 4800 feet per second (1460 m/s), over four times its speed in air. The distance the pulse has travelled can be determined from the measurement of the time it took to travel that distance.

Each pulse lasts anything from a few thousandths of a second to a few seconds depending upon the range of the particular sonar (the longer the range, the longer the pulse.) The pulses are emitted at intervals ranging from a fraction of a second to a few seconds or even minutes, again depending upon range. A typical shipboard echo sounder used for navigation has two range scales. On its shorter range it will measure depths up to 20 feet (6 m) in steps of a fraction of a foot. On its longer range it will measure depths up to 100 or more fathoms (1 fathom =6 feet=1.8 m).

The time interval, and therefore the range, can be measured by a rotating disc carrying a neon tube which flashes when the reflected pulse (the echo) is picked up. The disc rotates at a constant speed, carrying the neon tube past a fixed circular scale graduated in terms of distance. The neon tube is at the top alongside the zero mark when the pulse is transmitted. If the echo sounder is set to a maximum range of 100 fathoms the neon tube will be carried full circle that is, halfway round. The scale at this point is marked '50 fathoms', since the signal has travelled twice as far as the depth. In some units a permanent record is provided by a rotating stylus that darkens electrically sensitive paper when the echo is picked up. Other units have a cathode ray tube display similar to a TV screen. In all cases the distance is read directly from a scale which may be

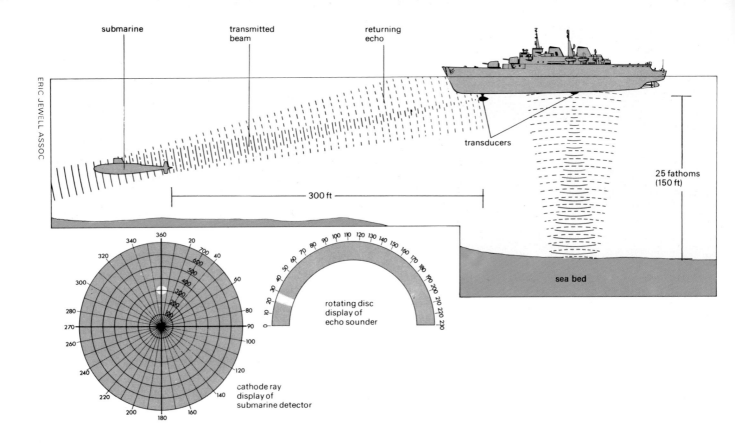

calibrated in feet, fathoms or metres.

All merchant and naval vessels carry an echo sounder, the simplest form of sonar used only to measure the depth of water. Fishing vessels carry a sonar that shows the depth and location of shoals of fish but naval and research sonar is considerably more powerful and complex. The sound pulses are concentrated into narrow beams by mechanical horns in a manner similar to that in loud-hailing equipment.

Alternatively, the beams can be produced by placing a series of transducers in a line along the ship's bottom. Although each transducer sends out signals in all directions, the signals radiated from the different transducers interfere constructively and destructively with each other. In one particular direction the interference effects are constructive, the signals add together, and a powerful beam is transmitted in that direction. In all other directions the signals interfere destructively and cancel each other out so that very little energy is transmitted in these directions. The direction in which the beam points can be changed easily and quickly by altering the electrical timing of the signals fed to different transducers.

The distance over which sound waves can travel in water is limited, and it is usual naval practice to send out sonar equipped helicopters which lower transducers below the sea's surface while hovering above it. Helicopters are also used to lay buoys equipped with transducers or microphones which radio any returning pulses back to the helicopter or nearby naval vessel. During the 1960s, extremely powerful transducers radiating millions of watts of sound energy were laid permanently on the edges of the continental shelf along the US coastline to provide long range detection of submarines. Shipborne, helicopter-borne and seabed sonar units can also be of the passive type in which no

Above: an anti-submarine ship equipped with sonar for echo sounding and submarine detection. The flat transducer towards the stern beams signals straight down to the bottom to find the depth, which is indicated in fathoms on a rotating disc display. The forward streamlined device scans through 360° to locate any submarines in the area. When one is detected it shows as a spot on the screen of a cathode ray tube, and its location is indicated.

Next page: the Decca Navigator gives readings which can be plotted directly on an overprinted chart. There are three dials; two readings are sufficient for a fix. Decca operates in Europe and other major traffic areas.

sound is transmitted. Instead, the transducers 'listen' for the engine, propeller and other sounds produced by submerged submarines.

One drawback of present day sonar is that no matter how sophisticated it is, it does only give a flash of light or a dark blob on a chart for each object detected—it does not give a detailed picture of the object. Research work indicates, however, that it might be possible to produce detailed pictures using sound waves and the technique of holography, previously used only with laser beams in air.

Another technique creates what is, in effect, an extremely long line of transducers. The fineness of the beam produced by such a line increases as the length of the line is increased, but this is limited by the size of the ship. This can be overcome by using a single transducer to transmit sound pulses over a long period as the ship steams along a path of, say, 1000 feet (300 m). The effect is the same as that of having an array of transducers 1000 feet (300 m) long.

LORAN AND DECCA

In the early 1900s, Marconi successfully demonstrated radio communication which was used initially to broadcast time signals for checking the chronometers (accurate clocks) carried on ships for astro-navigation. It was soon found that an aerial wound in a loop could detect the direction from which a radio wave was coming. The navigator now had eyes which could 'see' a radio beacon at night or in fog.

Radio waves travel nearly a million times as fast as sound waves, seven times round the Earth in a second. Nevertheless, shortly before World War II, echoes were being measured by radio. Using a directional aerial, generally in the form of a dish, distances and directions could be found and the results displayed on the face of a cathode ray tube. Thus radar enabled the mariner to see coastlines and other ships at night or in fog.

In recent decades, more money and effort has been expended on marine aids than in all the previous history of man. The lead line has been replaced by the echo sounder, which times the travel of sound waves from the hull of a ship to the seabed and back. During World War II the Loran and Decca Navigator systems came into use. These set up patterns over the earth comparable to the intersecting ripples of water when stones are thrown simultaneously into a pond. More recently, Omega, an ultra-long-range, very-low-frequency system has been developed.

All these systems work on the same principle, though there are practical differences between them. If two radio transmitters send out the same signal, say a continuous tone, the two wave motions will coincide with each other—that is, they will be in phase—along certain lines. These lines form a hyperbolic pattern around the transmitters. A ship picking up the signals exactly in phase must therefore be on one of these lines, which are marked on charts. To give a precise fix, signals from another pair of stations must be compared, the hyperbolic lines from which are also marked. Combining the two gives a unique position, once the lines involved are known.

This is the principle of the Decca system, which uses additional lane-identification signals transmitted from the ground stations every minute to give a unique fix. These drive automatic counters on board the ship, so that a continuous readout of position is displayed.

The basic Loran system uses pulses instead of continuous wave transmissions, giving rather less information but a greater accuracy at long distances; the Loran C system combines both. A limited system called Consol, giving direction details only, is used by yachtsmen.

The most recent system involves the use of satellites which orbit the Earth, broadcasting details of their orbits by means of a signal code which is changed by remote control from the ground as the orbit alters. As the satellite moves across the sky, the rate of change of its Doppler shift varies—its distance from the ship varies most rapidly when it is close to the horizon, and least when it is overhead. The orbit and Doppler information are fed into a computer on board the ship, which calculates the ship's position.

Recent increases in shipping traffic has led to the introduction of 'one way' lanes at sea, for example in the Strait of Dover, and port control systems using radar to watch vessels are now coming into use.

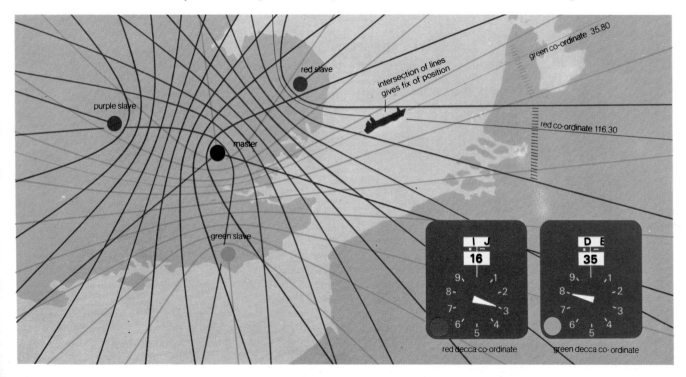

SAFETY, SALVAGE

After the 1840s British canals were allowed to fall into disuse; economic conditions forced families to live on their boats. This picture was taken in 1913. Brilliant British engineers built canals, then railways; one hopes that the railways will not also be abandoned.

AND ENGINEERING

LIGHTHOUSES AND LIGHTSHIPS

Until the introduction of lighthouses the usual way to mark the entrance to harbours or the presence of rocks or sandbanks was by means of a beacon, made up of a pile of stones or wooden spars. These simple warning devices are still used in small harbours, and more elaborate structures such as masts and pillars are widely used.

The first lighthouse of which there is any record was the Pharos of Alexandria (in Egypt), a huge structure built by Ptolemy in the third century BC. It has been estimated that the tower was built on a base 100 feet (30.5 m) square and was 450 feet (137 m) high. The Pharos survived until about AD 1200, when it was destroyed by an earthquake; it gave its name to *pharology*, the science of lighthouse building.

The Romans built many notable lighthouses, such as that at Ostia (the chief port for Rome) and others in Spain and France and at Dover. Following the fall of the Roman empire, navigational aids, along with many other aspects of that civilization, fell into disuse. Once again it was left to individual ports to set up and maintain their own lights. One drawback was that a lighthouse is undiscriminating in its aid to ships, and a port with a lighthouse was an easy target for attacking ships. This restricted the use of lighthouses to peacetime, which hampered their development for many years.

From about the eleventh century onwards the increase in sea trading led to a revival of interest in lighthouse construction. Progress was slow, but in England and Europe from about 1600 onwards there was an increase in lighthouse building culminating in the great era of lighthouse construction in the eighteenth and nineteenth centuries.

Illuminants

The most important feature of a lighthouse is its light, and the efficiency of the lights has increased as technology has advanced. The first lights burned wood, which had the drawback of burning too quickly. Coal and candles were also used, but coal gave off so much smoke that soot collected on the lantern panes and blocked the light. The problem with candles was that it was difficult to produce a satisfactory level of illumination no matter how many candles were used.

Lighthouse illumination did not become really efficient until the early 1780s when the Swiss engineer Aime Argand invented the type of oil burner which bears his name. This lamp used a circular wick, surrounded by a glass chimney which created a central, upward draught of air to assist the burning. This lamp produced a steady smokeless flame of high intensity, and it remained the principal source of light for over 100 years.

The Argand burner was adapted for use in domestic gas lighting and gas lighting technology in turn contributed to the next major advance in oil burners for lighthouses. The Argand lamp used a wick from which the oil vaporized for burning, but in 1901 Arthur Kitson produced a burner in which the oil was vap-

orized in a copper tube placed above the mantle (adapted from a gas mantle). The vapour then passed from the coiled tube to be burnt in the mantle, like gas. The oil was vaporized by the heat from the mantle, and a blowlamp was used to heat the coil before the lamp was lit. The Kitson design was improved by David Hood in 1921, and this type of burner is still widely used today where electric lighting is not practical. Many unattended lights burn acetylene gas.

Electric lighting was first tried in the South Foreland light on the Kent coast in 1858, using a carbon arc lamp, and this experiment was followed in 1862 by the installation of arc lamps at the Dungeness light, also in Kent. Arc lamps did not, however, prove satisfactory for lighthouses and little use was made of them.

The first use of electric filament lamps was also at the South Foreland light, in 1922, and many lighthouses are now operating with electric lights, either filament lamps or high pressure xenon lamps. The power is supplied from the local mains where possible, or else by diesel powered generators.

The third and most famous Eddystone light was designed by John Smeaton and completed in 1759, using a hydraulic cement invented by Smeaton, and with the stone blocks dovetailed together for strength. Erosion of the rock on which it was built necessitated its replacement by the present light which was built nearby, using an even more complex dovetailing

arrangement than Smeaton's, which was dismantled and re-erected on Plymouth Hoe as a memorial to him.

Where a suitable rock foundation is unavailable, such as where the hazard to be marked is a sandbank or coral reef, the light may be built on steel piles or concrete filled caisson foundations. The light towers of these are often of open steel frame construction.

Lighthouses are usually equipped with some form of siren or horn which is sounded in foggy or misty weather, and may be controlled by an automatic electronic fog detector. In some manned lighthouses explosive fog signals are still used, typically going off at five minute intervals.

Light vessels

The first light vessel (lightship) to go into service was moored near the Nore buoy in the Thames Estuary in 1731, and was found to be of great benefit by ship owners, who willingly subscribed to her upkeep. The lighting consisted of two ship's lanterns mounted 12 feet (3.7 m) apart on a cross beam on the single mast.

The light vessel was put on station by Robert Hamblin, who thought that navigation suffered from the difficulty of distinguishing one lighthouse from another, and considered that light vessels should be moored at dangerous points around the coast, using different arrangements of lanterns to enable each station to be easily identified.

The Nore vessel was placed on station against the wishes of Trinity House, the England lighthouse authority, who considered that lights which were only candles or oil lights would be ineffective as a guide to shipping. Despite these objections the King granted a patent for the light vessel, to run for 14 years from July 1730.

Following the immediate success of the Nore vessel, Trinity House became worried that light vessels would become so numerous as to upset the lighthouse system and eventually succeeded in persuading the King to revoke the patent in May 1732. The vessel had proved such a success, however, that it was impossible to remove it. Trinity House therefore obtained a patent in perpetuity and granted a lease for 61 years to Hamblin. After this initial breakthrough light vessels became accepted as valuable aids to navigation, but no other country tried them until 1800, and the first to be used in the USA did not go on station until 1820.

Optical systems

The development of efficient light sources led naturally to the development of reflector systems, because without some form of beam projection much of the intensity of the light is wasted. The three main groups of optical systems used in lighthouses are the catoptric (reflective), dioptric (refractive) and the catadioptric (reflective and refractive).

The first parabolic reflector was designed in 1752 by William Hutchinson, made up of small squares of mirrored glass set in plaster of Paris. The parabolic reflector is placed behind the light source and the rays of light are reflected parallel to the axis of the reflector and emerge as a beam of light. Reflectors made from a hand-beaten composition of copper and silver soon replaced the heavy glass reflectors, and by 1800 they were standard equipment in lighthouses.

The use of a reflector increased the power of the light signal by about 350 times, and as the problem of beam projection had thus been overcome the question of individual light characteristics for each lighthouse could be dealt with. This question arose because ship owners often complained that although lighthouses were useful, it was difficult to tell one from another as they all emitted the same signal.

This problem was solved by arranging reflectors in different positions on a frame and revolving it, producing group flashings (two or three flashes in quick succession, followed by a period of darkness, then the flashes again).

The most important development in lighthouse engineering was the Fresnel lens, invented by Augustin Fresnel in 1822. This is a dioptric lens, and has a central 'bullseye' lens surrounded by concentric rings of prismatic glass, each ring projecting a little way beyond the previous one. The overall effect of this arrangement is to refract (bend) into a horizontal beam most of the rays of light from a central lamp. Further reflecting elements may be placed above and below the refracting prisms to form a catadioptric arrangement.

Sometimes two lenses are placed one above the other, with a light at the centre of each, and this is called a bi-form optic. Many refinements have been made to Fresnel's original design, but the basic principle is essentially the same today.

Improved methods of producing and finishing glass, and the development of plastics, have made it possible to reduce the size and weight of optical systems. This, together with the improvement in light sources, has enabled more efficient and compact apparatus to be produced.

Construction

Most lighthouses are built of stone or precast concrete, and some are built many miles off shore. The Eddystone light, for example, stands on a rock in the English Channel some 13 miles (21 km) from Plymouth. The present structure is the fourth to be built on the site, and was completed in 1881. The original was a wooden tower, built in 1698 by Henry Winstanley who was at the light in 1703 when it was washed away during a severe storm. The second one, also of wood, was built by John Rudyerd in 1708 and survived until 1755 when it burned down.

In the United Kingdom, light vessels have no means of propulsion and have to be towed to and from stations. Each vessel remains on station for a three year period before being put into dry dock and overhauled. Many

98 other countries use self-propelled light vessels, includ-

Far left top: a drawing of
the original Eddystone
light. Henry Winstanley,
who designed it, died
when it was swept away
by a storm in 1703.
Below: part of the
machinery for rotating the
optics at the South Stack
lighthouse, Anglesey,
North Wales.
Left: the Dungeness
lighthouse, built in 1960.
The tower comprises 21
interlocking pre-cast
concrete rings which are
reinforced by steel wires
running under tension from
top to bottom. The
honeycomb section houses
the electric foghorn.
Above: one of four
lightships marking the
Goodwin Sands, a
dangerous stretch of
shifting sand near the
Strait of Dover.

ing the USA and Germany.

The invention of the parabolic reflector made light vessel identification much easier, but the main problem was keeping the light steady as the ship moved in the waves and wind.

The solution was to mount the optic above a set of gimbal bearings and counterbalance it with a weight below the bearings, so that the optic would remain upright as the ship moved.

The lighting system now used in light vessels is multicatoptric, consisting of eight parabolic reflectors mounted in pairs, one above the other, with an electric filament lamp in each. These reflectors are mounted on a frame which is rotated by a small electric motor. By varying the angular position of the reflectors and the speed of rotation of the frame it is possible to achieve single, double, triple and quadruple flashing lights.

SEA RESCUE

In the West, the first steps towards establishing sea rescue services were taken at the end of the 18th century, although by that time the Chinese had already been operating 'red boats' (specially built rescue boats) for several hundred years. Initial efforts were concentrated on building 'unsinkable' open boats, the first lifeboats, which were fitted with buoyancy tanks to keep them afloat. A boat of this type was successfully tested in France in 1765 and another was constructed in Britain in 1785. In the USA a lifeboat equipped with hydrogen filled buoyancy tanks was designed and constructed in 1816. This 'hydrogen lifeboat' was most commonly used as a ship's lifeboat.

Despite Britain's long maritime history it was not until 1824 that the first national organization for saving life at sea was formed. It was founded by Sir William Hillary in London, and known as the 'National Institution for the Preservation of Life from Ship-wreck', now the Royal National Lifeboat Institution (RNLI). Nowadays most European seafaring nations have some system for rescue at sea, whether operated by volunteers, the government or the armed forces. In Britain the lifeboat service is a voluntary one, the service being financed wholly by voluntary contributions and the great majority of crew members being volunteers who earn their living from other forms of employment.

Techniques

There are three basic methods of sea rescue—from a boat, from the air or from the shore. Rescue from the shore, often involving the use of breeches buoy apparatus is in Britain the responsibility of the coastguards. The Royal Navy and the RAF operate helicopters and the RNLI has a fleet of some 250 lifeboats. Rescue by helicopter can be quicker than by lifeboat, and if the rescued person is injured minutes may be vital. Life-

boats are able to stay out longer without refuelling and can take people from vessels which helicopters are unable to approach because of masts, rigging or fires: they are also better able to effect searches and rescues at night.

The essence of sea rescue is co-ordination. The casualty will normally attract attention either by radio or by firing distress flares. Other vessels may be able to help, but usually the coastguard receives the message or spots the flares and immediately alerts the appropriate rescue service. Most commonly this will be the lifeboat, perhaps with helicopter assistance. On long searches, where a vessel is reported missing, fixed-wing aircraft may help.

Lifeboats are normally based in one place and may lie afloat, be launched down a slipway or transported on a carriage down to the sea. The carriage launch (which is still performed by horses in parts of the Netherlands) uses specially designed tractors with watertight engines. The tractors may be submerged up to the driver's neck without stalling, as the air intake and exhaust pipes are extended above this level. In some countries, Norway for example, there are cruising lifeboats which accompany fishing fleets, and these have living accommodation on board.

Once at the scene of the casualty the coxswain of the lifeboat must quickly sum up the situation and decide which equipment will best help him. The main purposes of lifeboat equipment are to help a lifeboat to reach a casualty, to allow survivors to be taken off, to maintain communications with other vessels, aircraft and with the shore, and to give protection to the survivors and the crew. One of the great advances in sea rescue has been in communications. To maintain liaison between shore, sea and air, VHF and MF radio equipment is used.

The echo sounder, which tells a coxswain the exact depth of water under his boat, and the radio direction finder are among the items of electronic equipment. For some years after the invention of radar no sets were available for boats so low in the water as lifeboats, but radar is nowadays another standard fitting.

One of the most important pieces of equipment in helicopter rescue is the winch, for on this depends the lives of the crewmen and the casualty. Both helicopters and lifeboats carry first aid equipment and stretchers. Their men are protected by modern waterproof clothing, helicopter crews wearing helmets and lifeboat crews wearing life-jackets with a whistle and a light in case they should be washed overboard. Certain lifeboat crew members are also trained to carry out rescue work as swimmers wearing wet suits.

Lifeboats

Some of the modern lifeboat's equipment is traditional and has been proved by years of experience. The drogue, a hooped canvas cone streamed from the stern of the boat to steady her when she is running before a sea, and the breeches buoy are familiar items. To

Opposite page: the survivor's eye view of air-sea rescue. Above: The Cromer lifeboat puts to sea. Although it reduces their efficiency, the propellers are located in tunnels in the hull to protect them from damage during launch.

operate a breeches buoy, a device for bringing people from the casualty to shore or to the lifeboat, a line is fired from a rocket gun. Once secured, the crew works the buoy, with a survivor in it, to and fro along the fixed line by means of veering lines.

Recent constructional development of lifeboats has brought several completely new concepts. Designs have always been tied to the requirements of strength and ability to stand the worst weathers, as lifeboats put to sea when other vessels are seeking shelter. This has meant the incorporation of airtight buoyancy compartments in the hulls, so that if the hull is holed in several places, the lifeboat will remain afloat. One of the great controversies, which raged until recently, concerned self-righting—the ability of a boat to right herself in the event of capsize. Self-righting lifeboats of the last century were not liked by many crews, as the main buoyancy for righting was provided by high end boxes. These could not be built too high, otherwise they obstructed vision, so the boats had to be kept fairly narrow, reducing their initial stability and increasing the tendency to capsize.

Modern self-righting lifeboats have even greater stability than the non-self-righters designed between the Wars, and rely on the buoyant force provided by watertight compartments, including the engine casing and superstructure. Although the first boats to have this sort of righting arrangement also had a system of water ballast transfer, this is no longer necessary since watertight cabins and additional closed watertight doors have been introduced. A second departure from conventional designs has been new hull forms which have greatly increased the speeds of lifeboats.

Saving life at sea transcends international boundaries and co-operation between countries is as great, if not greater than in many other scientific fields. Designs and techniques are developed and discussed at international conferences, and it was at such a conference that the United States showed their 44 ft (13.4 m) steel hulled lifeboat. Capable of speeds of about 15 knots, she is exceptionally manoeuvrable and lies afloat. There are several of this type of lifeboat in service around the coasts of Britain and Ireland and more are being built. The 52 ft (15.9 m) 'Arun' class lifeboat, initally built in wood, is now being construced in GRP (glass reinforced plastic or glass fibre). This new material for large lifeboats had to be stringently studied before acceptance. Boats of this class have speeds in excess of 20 knots, are self-righting and, like the 44 foot lifeboats, lie afloat. They have double skinned hulls, the spaces between the inner and outer skins being filled with expanded polyurethane foam which keeps the lifeboat afloat even if all 26 of the watertight compartments are holed. The superstructure is made of welded aluminium and the seats in the wheelhouse for the five crew members are equipped with safety belts. The vessel can be controlled either from the wheelhouse or from a 'flying' bridge situated above the wheelhouse. Access

Above: the winchman and a survivor being winched into the helicopter from a rubber dinghy. Top right: a Sea King helicopter of the Royal Navy rescues the six crew members of the Italian freighter Giovanna Assenzo. *The ship radioed for help 110 miles (177 km) south of Malta, and later sank. The helicopter has a range of more than 500 miles (805 km).*

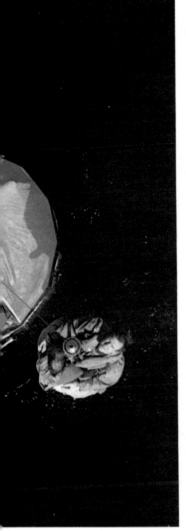

Above: an inshore rescue boat operated by the RNLI. It is driven by an outboard motor and is ideal for rescue in shallow waters.

to the wheelhouse is through a 'coffer dam' entrance which has two doors, like an airlock, to prevent flooding if the vessel should capsize. The lifeboat is powered by two 375 hp marine diesel engines. One of the limitations of these boats is that they cannot be launched down slipways. Coastlines vary greatly, and in many places there will be no harbour with a sufficient depth of water at all states of the tide to moor a lifeboat afloat, and so a slipway is necessary. To protect the screws and prevent cavitation a certain hull form, with propellers in tunnels, has until recently, been found necessary and such a design precludes great speed.

Inshore rescue

One of the most important recent innovations in sea rescue techniques has been the development of inshore lifeboats. Increasing numbers of people in all developed countries are taking their leisure on the sea, and naturally some of them get into difficulties. Small dinghies, yachts, swimmers and children on air beds may all need very quick assistance and to meet this growing demand inshore lifeboats were introduced. International co-operation is again helping to push forward research into this field. A most successful boat is the sophisticated 'Atlantic 21' developed by the RNLI.

Inshore lifeboats can be launched very quickly from a beach and are capable of high speeds once in the water. The 'Atlantic 21' can reach about 29 knots, and her twin outboard motors and glass fibre hull with inflatable sponsons make her a very able craft. Self-righting is achieved by means of an air bag fitted on a frame over the stern. If the lifeboat should capsize, the air bag can be inflated from the upturned position, the stern is pushed up and the boat rights itself. Smaller 16 ft (4.9 m) inflatable boats, ideal for rescue operations in shallow waters, operate all around the coasts of Britain and Ireland.

MARINE SALVAGE

Marine salvage is the recovery of objects lost or damaged in the oceans, and the salvaging techniques may apply also to lakes and rivers. In modern times many objects ranging from treasure to hydrogen bombs, as well as wrecked ships, have been recovered by salvage operations.

Grounded ships

A ship which has run aground may seem, at first, to be a simple salvage job, but each salvage operation is different, and ingenuity is always important. If a ship has simply run aground, it may be necessary only to wait for the next high tide and pull her afloat again, but this depends upon the circumstances. If a ship goes aground in a rocky, treacherous terrain, her hull may be broken when the tide goes out. If the hull suffers some damage from running aground, it may be possible to make temporary repairs, with steel or wooden patches which the water pressure will help to hold in place when the ship is afloat.

If a vessel has been driven high aground by winds and waves, it may still be possible to refloat her by lightening ship. Freight, fixtures and even the ship's super-structure may be removed and transferred to waiting barges, but it is important to anchor the ship in the direction of deep water before lightening begins, so that in her lightened condition she does not go further aground. The ship's own anchors, as well as salvage anchors, can be placed in deep water and a strain kept on the lines to assist in refloating, and tug-boats are used if available.

Sunken ships

Whether sunken ships can be salvaged depends upon a combination of factors: depth of water, size of the ship, weather conditions, availability of equipment, estimated cost, and so on. The larger the ship to be salvaged the more difficult the job will be at a given depth, because the amount of lift available from the different types of equipment used is limited.

Effective salvage operations only became possible in the last hundred years or so, because of the technology needed to do the job. Divers are nearly always needed to assist the salvaging, the hardhat diving suit being best suited to stationary work such as may be needed on a wreck. Where manoeuvrability is required, the aqualung [scuba gear] is needed.

If a wreck lies in shallow water, it may be possible to locate it from aircraft. Underwater television cameras are also used, operated from surface vessels or from submersibles. Among the most useful devices are radar and sonar. The fathometer is a variation of sonar which is used by oceanographers to map the shape of the ocean's floor; the device can also be used by the salvage team to detect unusual shapes which could indicate the location of a wreck. These methods run into difficulties if a vessel has sunk in an area where the ocean floor is naturally rough, as it will be difficult to distinguish between natural and unnatural projections.

Once the wreck is located, the work of the divers begins. Mechanical lifting by crane, cable and so forth is still the most common method, as it has been since the invention of the diving suit made it possible to attach cables and chains to the hulk. The laying of cables is done so that the sunken vessel is cradled by supporting gear which leads to the surface; the cables are frequently positioned by dredgers, with the assistance of divers, and the chief considerations are the size of the hulk, the power and buoyancy of the surface vessels and the unpredictability of the weather. If the cables are improperly positioned or if the weight of the hulk shifts as it is being lifted, weeks of work may go for nothing; the stricken vessel may break its back or slip out of the matrix of cable and go back to the bottom.

A sunken vessel is likely to be mired in mud at the bottom, and the effect is a powerful force of static friction or suction. The force required to break the suction will be many times the force required to lift the vessel once it is free, with the result of a sudden increase in the rate of the vessel's motion. This can break the ship's hull or at least cause it to be difficult to control. Ingenious methods have been devised to deal with this problem. Cables from the positive and negative terminals on a dynamo [generator] on the surface vessel can be directed to two sides of a sunken hull so that they become positive and negative electrodes. When the power is turned on, the water between the electrodes acts as a conductor; electrolysis results, and the water is broken up into hydrogen and oxygen; hydrogen bubbles attach themselves to the hull, displacing the mud and destroying the static friction.

With wooden vessels an alternate procedure is followed: the divers direct jet streams of water containing pellets of iron and magnesium into the sediment. The salt in the water sets off an electrolyzing reaction so that hydrogen bubbles displace the mud.

Other lifting methods

Mechanical lifts are often aided by other devices, such as pontoons. These are empty metal drums which are flooded, sunk, arranged around the hulk and finally pumped free of water, with compressed air, buoyancy resulting. Pontoons were developed especially for rescuing submarines.

Compressed air is often used without pontoons. Apertures and leaks are sealed by divers so that the vessel becomes relatively airtight; most sea-going vessels have been constructed in compartment form anyway, so it is often not necessary to seal up the whole of a wreck before pumping in compressed air.

Mechanical lifting can be aided by the tides as well. Partially flooded vessels are attached to the sunken hull at low tide, and pumped free of water as the tide rises, providing extra lift. This method is particularly successful where the lifting equipment is insufficiently powerful for the job on hand.

Polyurethane foam has been used to raise vessels. Polyurethane components are sent down in a hose to a

mixing chamber which divers have installed near the wreck. Another agent which has a low boiling point is also sent to the chamber, and the materials are mixed and expelled with pressurized nitrogen. The low-boiling agent volatilizes because of the sudden decrease in pressure, and a froth of polyurethane bubbles is produced inside the hull. The bubbles cure to form a rigid, cellular material; each cubic foot of this foam weighs 2 lb (0.907 kg) and displaces 64 lb (29 kg) of water. Polyurethane beads or pressure-injected spheres are even better, because they are easier to remove from the recovered hull than solid foam. These are pumped into the hull through a pipe. The pressure-injected spheres are 11 inches (27 cm) in diameter providing 30 lb (13.6 kg) of buoyancy; they are pressurized to synchronize with ambient pressure at a given depth and are equipped with valves which allow internal pressure to adjust as necessary. The advantages of these methods over compressed air is that the wreck does not have to be made airtight by the divers, and that the polyurethane materials provide buoyancy whose thrust is entirely upwards.

The prop wash is an elbow-shaped aluminium tube which fits on the transom of a boat. The wash from the ship's propeller is directed through it to the sand at the bottom, so that digging operations which used to take days for divers can sometimes be accomplished in a few minutes. The air lift is used to recover small objects. It is an open-ended pipe; a hose from the surface supplies compressed air to a perforated chamber at the lower end of the pipe. The air bubbles rush upwards, creating suction which carries small objects with it.

Seaprobe
Future development of salvage techniques will be in the area of deep water salvage using submersible craft directed from the surface. *Seaprobe*, for example, is a vessel of 2000 ton displacement, which is controlled from the surface by means of television equipment. *Seaprobe* has a drilling rig capable of handling a pipe string instead of cable; pipe has strength and rigidity for exerting torque and pumping water at the higher pressures found at depth. A television probe is used at the end of the pipe for searching for wrecks. Once the prize is discovered, if it is relatively small, such as a downed satellite, it can be retrieved by a steel trapeze trailing a wire bag or by large tongs also operated from the surface via television observation.

Left: wreckage is cleared from the Thames in 1946.
Above: a scuttled German battleship of World War 1 is raised in 1936. Eight airlocks were used.

Lifting larger objects from great depths is more difficult. Anything larger than 1000 tons must be cut into smaller pieces. Ordinary compressors used on surface vessels have an upper limit of 1000 psi (68.9 bar) and the pressure at 6000 ft (nearly 2 km), for example, is 3000 psi (207 bar). Seaprobe can produce quantities of greatly compressed air using a compressor with a water pump and an air receiver. The compressor delivers air to the chambered receiver, which has an automatic air-operated valve between it and the pipe. Water is fed into the pipe by a pump and the regulator monitors back pressure so that the air-to-water ratio is controlled. Each slug of air is followed by a slug of water, momentarily decreasing the back-pressure so that another slug of air can follow it. The water rides down on the air, further compressing it with its own weight and the weight of all the water and air in the pipe above it. A chamber at the lower end of the pipe receives both air and water; the air rises to be trapped in the chamber, and the water is thrust out into the sea. Thus greatly compressed air is available to do work at greater pressure than could be attained from an ordinary compressor. Pontoons and sunken drydocks can then be used at depth, though the highly compressed air must be bled off as the recovered object ascends.

Destroying wrecks
Salvage companies are often asked to destroy or remove a wreck rather than to recover it; during wartime scuttled or sunken ships often blocked ports, for example. Sometimes the wreck is recovered and towed to deeper water to be sunk again but explosives are also used. A ring of explosives is placed around the wreck and detonated; tons of water suddenly converge on the hulk, crushing it. Successively smaller rings of explosives are detonated until even the most obstinate hulk will 'disappear'.

DREDGING

Dredgers, also called dredges, are floating excavation machines used for keeping harbours, canals and navigable waterways free from excessive accumulations of mud and silt. In modern times several other functions have developed, including supplying material for land reclamation, collecting gravel and sand for the construction industry, and mining diamonds, gold, tin and other minerals from the inshore sea bed.

Centuries ago dredging was carried out by the 'bag and spoon' method, using manual labour. The forerunners of modern dredgers were developed in the middle of the seventeenth century, and were powered by horses until the advent of the steam engine. By 1900 dredgers of the bucket, grab and dipper type were in use. In the present century the power source is usually a diesel engine connected directly to the machinery or operating a generator which produces electricity.

The twentieth century has seen two important developments in dredging technology. Firstly, with the aid of surveying techniques and modern electronic navigation aids, dredging has become a more precise operation where necessary; secondly, the efficient suction method of dredging is rendering older types of dredgers obsolescent, except for very small operations where very hard materials have to be removed.

Bucket dredgers

The bucket dredger was for many years the most common type, and many such machines are still in use today. It is essentially a chain-and-bucket conveyor, strung on a frame called a ladder, which is hydraulically raised and lowered at the appropriate angle to the bottom. The bucket dredger is usually not self-propelled, and must be towed to the site by a tugboat. It is used in conjunction with hopper barges, which haul the dredged material out to sea to dump it. The bucket dredger is secured with anchors, and can be manoeuvred over its working area to a limited extent by pulling in one anchor cable and letting out another. The most serious disadvantage of the bucket dredger is that when it is used in shipping channels it tends to be in the way of commerce.

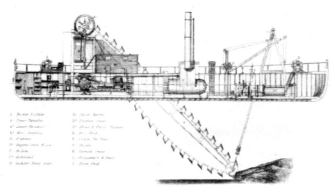

Above: a drawing from a 19th century encyclopedia of a steam-powered chain and bucket dredger, not different in principle from those used today.

Grab and dipper dredgers

The dipper is a mechanical shovel which pivots on a boom, and the grab is the familiar 'clamshell', or pair of hinged jaws for grabbing bulk materials, suspended by cables from the end of a boom. Grab dredgers and dipper dredgers are more manoeuvrable than bucket dredgers, and can work in awkward corners and close to quay walls. Some of them are self-propelled and have their own hoppers, so that they can haul their own spoil to the dumping ground. During the dredging part of their operation, they are usually secured by lines fore and aft; it is the deck winches and the derricking of the boom which provide the manoeuvrability. They are usually fitted with spuds—extendable legs which reach to the bottom—to provide stability and leverage against the material being dredged.

Suction dredgers

There are several types of suction dredger, all making use of the centrifugal pump. The impeller of such a pump causes suction by its spinning action which pulls water and solids up from the bottom through an airtight tube. The discharge of the tube is directed into the centre of the spining impeller, and the discharge vent of the pump is around the outside of the casing. Some dredgers have several pumps going at once. The tube can be made flexible with airtight fittings at the joints.

Where the material to be dredged is soft and granular, such as sand or gravel, no further refinements are needed, but for other applications the suction device has been adapted for use with cutters, drag-arms and scrapers ('dustpans') to loosen the material or break it up. The sucking end of the suction tube is located near the mechanical device in order to collect the spoil as it is broken up.

The suction drag-arm vessel has a conventional seagoing hull, and the drag-arm is mounted underneath it. The hoppers for the spoil are built into the hull as well. The cutterhead dredger has a revolving cutter at the end of a ladder; the cutter chops impacted material out of the bottom so that the suction device can handle it.

Some suction dredgers have spuds for stability in relatively shallow water; some have floating pipelines which can be extended some distance from the ship for dumping the spoil as soon as it is sucked up. Suction dredgers can be fitted with chutes in such a way that they deliver the spoil to waiting barges or dockside dump trucks. A suction dredger used in a land reclamation project can suck the spoil from the bottom and 'shoot' the solids straight over a nearby embankment into the area to be filled in.

The largest modern dredgers have hopper capacities of around 12,000 tons, and capacities up to 30,000 tons are expected soon. Larger dredging operations are made necessary by the large size of modern super-tankers, which require large-scale excavation of dock-side waters at oil terminals.

Above: a chain and bucket dredger of the type used to remove silt from canal and river bottoms. It can be manipulated to some extent by means of the anchor chains. Left: a tin dredger 394 feet long and weighing 2800 tons. The ladder is raised by means of cables.

DOCKS

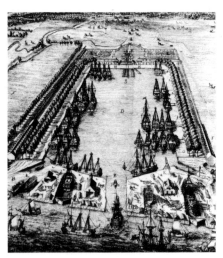

Above: the Howland Great Wet Dock near Deptford, later incorporated into the Surrey commercial dock system, was built in the 17th century. Note rows of trees planted as windbreaks.

For many centuries sea traders relied solely on the shelter afforded by natural harbours, inlets and river estuaries in order to load or discharge, victual or repair their ships. While lying at anchor, their vessels were at the mercy, not only of wind and tide, but of bands of marauders to whom they were easy prey. The need for protection from such threats led to the establishment of basins or wet docks where sailing ships could be fitted out in safety and where their cargoes could be dealt with in relative security.

The word 'dock', which to this day is used fairly loosely to describe a variety of places where ships are berthed, was first used to describe 'an artificial basin filled with water and enclosed by gates' during the second half of the sixteenth century, a period of considerable expansion in maritime trade. One of the first recorded enclosed dock basins was the Howland Great Wet Dock which was built on the south bank of the River Thames in the seventeenth century. In the late eighteenth and nineteenth centuries the great dock-building period began in earnest, often closely associated with canal and railway-building ventures. This was also the period of the first iron steamships but the tremendous growth in ship sizes since those days has made many early docks obsolete.

The provision of gates at dock entrances is necessary because of the large tidal range which would otherwise cause the basins to have insufficient depth of water at low tide. In many countries the rise and fall of the tide is so insignificant that docks can be completely tidal. For example, in Melbourne, Australia, spring tides (those with the greatest range) rise less than 3 ft (1 m), in Rotterdam about 6.5 ft (2 m); and in Boston, USA, about 10 ft (3 m).

In Britain, however, with its large tidal ranges, most major dock systems are enclosed. The most notable exception to this is at Southampton where all dock berths are tidal, and where the effects of a 13 ft (4 m) tidal range are minimized by a phenomenon known as the 'double tide', which gives six hours of high water a day. An extreme example of a tidal range which makes enclosed docks imperative occurs in the Severn Estuary, where Bristol, for instance, experiences a maximum variation of almost 49 ft (15 m) between high and low water.

Lock entrances

The dimensions of the lock-pit inevitably govern the maximum size of vessel which can enter an enclosed dock. With the trend towards larger ships in recent years, the constraints of existing entrance locks have become a problem. The largest lock in Britain, at Tilbury, is 1000 ft (305 m) long and 110 ft (33.5 m) wide, with a depth of $45\frac{1}{2}$ ft (14 m), whereas the largest container ships, now operating between Europe and the Far East, are 950 ft (290 m) long overall, 106 ft (32 m) in beam, and have a maximum draught of $42\frac{1}{2}$ ft (12 m). New entrance locks are being built to cater for vessels even larger than this. At the West Dock at Bristol a

lock measuring 1200 ft (366 m) long and 140 ft (43 m)
wide is being constructed to take ships of 75,000 tons
dead-weight, and developments at Le Havre in
France include a new lock 1312 ft (400 m) in length
and 219 ft (67 m) wide. This is claimed to be the world's
largest lock and is capable of accommodating a tanker
of 500,000 tons deadweight.

The operation of an entrance lock is basically simple.
By using a system of culverts and sluices, water is
allowed to pass from the dock into the lock with both
inner and outer gates shut. The water level, and with it
any ship in the lock, rises until it reaches dock level,
when the inner gates open and the ship moves into
dock. A departing vessel can then be penned in the
lock and lowered by allowing water in the lock to
escape through the outer sluices.

Dock layouts
Although certain cargoes such as coal or bulk grain
require specialized handling facilities, dock berths have
traditionally been multipurpose and vary little in
design, layout and equipment. Usually the quay apron
(the working area alongside ship) is equipped with
rail tracks both for cranes and railway wagons, and is
flush-surfaced to give access to road vehicles. Quay
cranes of three to five tons capacity at 80 ft (24 m) radius
are usually adequate for break-bulk general cargo
operations (where individual packages, drums, bales,
and so on are handled piecemeal using cargo trays,
nets, slings, or hooks) but cranes of greater capacity
are installed where heavier cargo, for example steel
traffic, is frequently dealt with. For even heavier items
many ports are equipped with floating cranes, often
with lifting capacities exceeding 100 tons.

marshalling area

unloading

container terminal: sea
units are unloaded dire
or stored in marshalling

dock enclosure (fixed water level)

lock gates for
use with small
ships to save water

roll-on roll-off ferry
for private vehicles

passenger terminals
and customs sheds

main lock gates retain water in dock
at higher level than outside

lighter-aboard-ship (LASH) sy
allows large ships to moor in ti
while tugs remove the lighters

open tidal water

dry dock for repair work

goods unloading

goods collection area
for road transport

transit sheds

rail access

road access

floating dock

JANECLARE

CHAELJOHN

Above left: a container being bottom-lifted. This container is not completely standardized; most containers can be top-lifted by means of standard holes, one in each corner, which permit the use of hydraulic 'twist-lock' devices.
Above: container handling at Tilbury Docks, London. This view is looking down the long boom of the travelling crane.

Transit sheds adjacent to the quay apron give temporary covered accommodation to cargo prior to its loading aboard ship or collection by road or rail vehicles. Modern sheds have the maximum possible unobstructed floor area so that mobile equipment such as fork lift trucks, platform trucks and mobile cranes can be used to carry and stack cargo. To the rear of the sheds, loading bays with road and rail access serve for the delivery of goods.

Container docks

The dramatic changes that have occurred in cargo transportation over the past ten years have, however, completely transformed the layout of modern terminals. These new techniques include containerization—the carriage of general goods in large containers of internationally standardized dimensions—and 'roll-on roll-off' employing vessels with bow, stern, or side doors through which wheeled freight is loaded and discharged.

A typical container-handling dock has a large area of land serving each berth, ideally 20 to 25 acres (8 to 10 hectares), for container marshalling. It does not normally have covered accommodation, except where container stuffing (packing) and unstuffing or Customs examination are carried out, although container warehouses have been constructed with their own internal gantry cranes for stacking.

Two or three giant gantry cranes, with lifting capacities of up to 40 tons, and capable of working a three-minute cycle (that is loading and unloading 20 containers an hour) may be provided to a berth. For large ocean-going container ships at least 1000 ft (305 m) of quay is allocated for each berth. Mobile handling equipment may include van carriers, which straddle, lift, carry and stack containers three high, tractors and trailers, or side- or front-loaders, each with similar lifting capacities. Alternatively, the gantry cranes may span the entire stacking area, carrying out all movements between ship, container stack, and inland transport.

With large container ships carrying 2000 or more containers and perhaps discharging half of these at one port and then loading a similar number, the operation of a container terminal is highly complex. For this reason computer control of container movements is widely used, and studies are already in hand with a view to the automation of future container berths, perhaps with fleets of 'robotugs' responding to radio signals.

Ferry terminals

Although many roll-on roll-off ferry terminals cater for passengers as well as freight and have passenger facilities of varying degrees of refinement, roll-on roll-off terminals consist mainly of a ramp, shore bridge, or linkspan on to which the ferry can open its doors, and a large marshalling area for the vehicles it carries. In some cases a simple concrete ramp built out from the quay wall is all that is necessary, but most shore bridges are tailor-made for the individual vessel using them, with electrically operated machinery able to compensate for the ferry's changing draught during loading operations. Like all very successful ideas roll-on roll-off is a simple concept and it has revolutionized the carriage of cargo on short sea routes.

Bulk terminals

The economics of transportation are resulting in the building of increasingly large vessels for bulk handling of raw materials but arrangements must be made to accommodate them. *Globtik Tokyo* and *Globtik London*, the largest tankers afloat, are 477,000 tons deadweight, 1243 ft (382 m) long, and have a draught of 92 ft 6 in (28 m). Oil tankers are usually brought to jetties sited in deep water but a relatively new system of loading and unloading uses what is known as single point mooring buoy or monobuoy mooring, linked by pipeline to the shore installations, and which is placed as far out to sea as is necessary.

Special dock facilities exist for other bulk traffics, iron ore being a prime example. Vessels of 100,000 tons or more are now regularly employed carrying ore to Europe from Australia, Brazil and Canada. Modern terminals such as the British Transport Docks Board's Port Talbot Harbour in South Wales work around the clock 365 days of the year when necessary; their transporter cranes fitted with 20-ton capacity grabs are capable of average discharge rates of 1800 tons an hour.

Dry docks and floating docks

At regular intervals all ships need to be inspected 'in the dry', and sometimes repaired. For this reason, most major ports are equipped with dry, or graving docks; slipways being used for smaller ships.

Dry docks, which usually take one ship at a time, are simply basins which are capable of being pumped dry to leave a ship supported by an arrangement of 'keel blocks', so that work can be carried out on the hull, propellers, or rudder. The procedure for drydocking a ship is a precise affair and may take several hours; with the dock flooded the gate is opened and the ship enters, then the gate is closed and pumping begins. Accurate positioning is vital as the ship settles on the blocks, prearranged to fit her hull, and to facilitate this, modern dry docks are usually fitted with guidance systems. In many international ports dry docks are being provided for the largest tankers afloat or planned: the port of Rotterdam already has a dry dock 1350 ft (412 m) long, which can accommodate 500,000-ton tankers, and the construction of a super dry dock for 700,000-tonners will be carried out at Kiel over the next two years.

The purpose of a floating dock is the same as that of a conventional dry dock, only the method of getting the ship out of the water differs. Ballast tanks are used to raise the submerged dock towards the surface and with it the ship to be repaired.

A large floating dock would have a lifting capacity of 20,000 tons, which would enable it to deal with ships of up to 70,000 tons deadweight. Such a dock, ordered recently for the Scandinavian port of Aalborg, will be 750 ft (228 m) long, 120 ft (37 m) wide between the inner walls and 148 ft (45 m) wide.

Below left: bulk handling of petroleum products is done by pumping it in and out of tanks.
Below: minesweepers in dry dock in Brest, France. The ships are carefully positioned and supported and the water pumped out of the dock. Dry docks are necessary for repairs below the waterline.

CANALS AND LOCKS

The term canal may be defined as any completely man-made open water channel, whether it is used for irrigation, land drainage, water supply or navigation. When we use the word nowadays, however, it is usually in the context of navigation by boats, although many canals may serve a secondary function as a drainage or water supply channel.

Canals are not to be confused with river navigations. Such rivers may range from natural channels which, because of their size, are navigable far inland, to those which have been improved and made navigable by the construction of artificial 'cuts' to bypass acute bends, shallows and rapids, together with the construction of many locks.

Locks

A boat on a canal or river, or entering a dock, may have to be passed from one level to another. The simplest device which can do this is a pound or chamber lock. The general form of the modern lock is that of an open-topped chamber, with watertight gates at each end. Once the boat is inside, the gates are shut and the water level in the lock then rises or falls (depending on whether the boat is ascending or descending). When the water in the chamber has reached the right level, the appropriate gate is opened to allow the boat to leave the lock.

Locks have a history of at least two thousand years, although the earliest were not pound locks. One factor limiting the navigability of rivers is the depth of water and to increase this, dams were often built. Part of each dam was removable, permitting boats to be winched upstream through the gap, or swirled downstream by the current. The removable part is called a flash lock: the entire structure, a navigation weir. Its use was two-fold: the impounded water not only increased upstream depths, but could also be released in a surge to assist vessels in shallow water downstream. Locks of this type existed in China 70 AD, and their use later spread as they were built into water-mill weirs as well. Although this reduced disputes between millers and boatmen, these could not be settled until the adoption of the pound lock, whose closed chamber minimizes the water loss from the higher level. In 984, the first known example of a pound lock was built in China, and was operated by raising or lowering gates at each end (now called guillotine gates). Europe's earliest pound lock which can be dated precisely was built in 1373 at Vreeswijk, Holland, and also had guillotine gates.

Most modern locks have an improved type of gate invented by Leonardo da Vinci in the fifteenth century for a canal in Milan, Italy. These gates turn on hinges, like doors, and each end of the lock has two such gates which meet to form a vee pointing upstream, giving them the name mitre gates. England's first pound locks with mitre gates were built in 1567 on the Exeter Canal.

One advantage of mitre gates is that since the vee shape points upstream, they are self sealing. When there is a difference in water level between one side and the other, the pressure holding the gates together is at its greatest.

Ancient locks were often built entirely of wood, but stone or brick chambers later became standard. Gates were usually of wood, lasting up to 50 years. To fill and empty the lock, hand-operated sluices were fitted to the gates, but it was later found that mounting these in conduits bypassing the gates gave a smoother water flow.

Where steep rises have to be negotiated, locks are built contiguously, with the upper gates of one acting as the lower gates of the next. The resulting structure is called a staircase and many examples exist from 'two-steps' (three sets of gates) to the mighty 'Neptune's Staircase' on the Caledonian Canal, Scotland, which consists of eight locks condensed into one structure with nine sets of gates.

Construction

Modern lock construction can readily be seen to represent a refinement of older types, with concrete usually used for the chamber and welded steel for the gates. Hydraulic power or electricity is used to operate the gates and sluices. As locks have grown in size to admit larger vessels, so, on canals, the problem of the water lost from higher to lower levels has increased. To overcome this, pumping may be employed, or economizer locks built. These have small reservoirs alongside the chamber to store some of the water emptied from it. This water is later used to refill the lock. The outstanding examples of this type are on the Rhine-Main-Danube Canal which will link Germany's waterways to those of southeastern Europe. Here, multiple-side-reservoirs allow savings of up to 60% of the lock water. The locks are 623 ft (190 m) long, 39 ft (12 m) wide and have rises up to 81 ft (25 m).

In the mid-nineteenth century, locks rarely had rises above 30 ft (9 m), but today's largest has a rise of 138 ft (42 m). This is at Ust-Kamenogorskiy, USSR, and lifts 1600 ton vessels past a hydroelectric dam on the River Irtish. The chamber, 328 ft (100 m) long and 56 ft (17 m) wide, takes about half an hour to fill or empty. The lower gate does not extend for the full height; it moves vertically to seal a 'tunnel' through which ascending vessels pass to enter the lock.

The Panama Canal also has large locks, especially remarkable as it was opened in 1914. These have mitre gates up to 82 ft (25 m) high and can accommodate vessels 1000 ft (305 m) long and 110 ft (34 m) wide taking only eight minutes to fill or empty.

Canal routes

The use of modern type locks on river navigations was widespread long before canals became popular. The reason for this was that to build over a high watershed involved major civil engineering works for which there was neither the expertise nor the capital available. Many early canals are called contour canals because

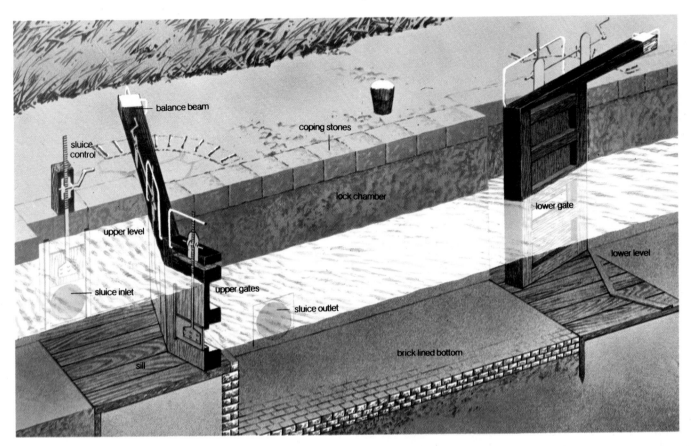

they follow a very devious course along the natural contours in an effort to avoid the cost of major earthworks, aqueducts or tunnels. Even so, such major works were impossible to avoid; equally unavoidable was the problem of supplying the summit, or highest level, of the canal with sufficient water to compensate for that used in lockage. Each boat, as it passes through such a canal, draws two lock chambers full of water away from the topmost level, one as it ascends and another as it descends, and more water will be required for larger lock chambers. To make the problem more difficult for the engineer, this demand for water arises at the precise point where it is most difficult to supply, being situated on an upland plateau.

The first true summit level canal was built in France to link the River Loire with the River Seine. This was the Canal de Briare, 21 miles (34 km) long with 40 locks to carry it over a 266 ft (81 m) summit level. Hugues Cosnier was the brilliant engineer responsible and from the day it was opened in 1642 his canal was a commercial success. As a prototype it paved the way for another far more ambitious work, that of the Canal du Midi which was built under the direction of Pierre Paul Riquet between 1671 and 1685 to link the Garonne at Toulouse with the Mediterranean. It is 149 miles (240 km) long and there are 99 locks which lift the canal over a 620 ft (189 m) summit level. Riquet went to amazing lengths to ensure that this high sum-

mit level had an adequate supply of water. To this end he drove nearly 40 miles (64 km) of feeder channels and built a huge dam at St Ferreol in the hills of the Massif Central.

History

When it was built in the 17th century, the Canal du Midi was the greatest work of civil engineering then existing and it served as a prototype for the world to copy. For example, Francis Egerton, Duke of Bridgewater, visited the Midi Canal while he was on a grand tour of the Continent, and what he saw there emboldened him to embark on the construction of the Bridgewater Canal from his estate at Worsley to Manchester, later extending it to the Mersey at Runcorn. This began the era of canal construction in England which lasted roughly from 1760 to 1830. First, the four great rivers of England, Mersey, Trent, Severn and Thames, were linked by a 'cross' of canals engineered by James Brindley and his assistants using the old contour canal principle. These canals were later supplemented by new and more direct routes of which the last was Thomas Telford's Birmingham and Liverpool Junction Canal which was completed in 1834. In contrast to Brindley's contour canals, the latter was surveyed and built on the 'cut and fill' technique adopted by the railway builders whereby the amount excavated in cuttings equals that required to raise the embankments.

This canal system of the English Midlands as

devised by Brindley and his successors played a key role in Britain's industrial revolution by providing an economical method of transport for goods in bulk, especially coal. Unfortunately, however, Brindley adopted as standard on his canals a lock chamber 70 ft (21 m) long but only 7 ft (2.1 m) wide which restricted their use to special canal 'narrow boats' of similar dimensions carrying only 30 tons. Doubtless it was the water supply problem that determined this slim gauge, but although it proved adequate for 18th century needs, it became quite inadequate in the 20th century. France, for example, considers a 350 ton barge the minimum economic size and when it is realized that both the 30 tonner and the 350 tonner cost the same in man hours to work through a canal, it becomes easy to understand the reason why the greatest part of England's canal system today is suitable only for pleasure craft.

Just as the Duke of Bridgewater was influenced by the example of the Canal du Midi, so, in turn, Americans and Canadians were influenced by the spate of canal construction in England. There was a certain time lag, for whereas in England canal construction reached its peak in 1792, in North America it did not begin seriously until 1816 when a number of waterways were constructed to provide better communication between the East Coast and the Middle West.

Canals today

With significant exceptions, the canal heyday in England and North America was brief. Perhaps because railways were specifically an English invention, the English speaking world seems to have lost interest in its canals with their coming in the 1830s. By assuming too readily that railways were the only answer to every transport need, many canals were allowed to fall into neglect and decay. This was not the case on the continent of Europe where both transport systems continued to develop side by side. It was realized that each form of transport was suited to certain traffic and that the particular role of the canal was in carrying low value bulk cargoes over long distances, provided it was capable of passing craft of sufficiently large tonnage. In Europe, therefore, certain trunk canal routes have been progressively enlarged over the years.

For example, the Brussels-Charleroi Canal, originally suitable for 400 ton craft when it was opened in 1895, has now been completely reconstructed to accept 1350 ton barges. Again, the Great North Holland Ship Canal, constructed between 1819 and 1825, enabled craft of 800 tons to reach Amsterdam, but thanks to recent reconstruction this figure has been raised to 2000 tons.

Another example is the Rhine-Danube Canal which

The Rochdale Canal, in Lancashire. Britain's canal system has not been maintained or improved over the years. In France, waterborne traffic increased from 76 million tons to 106 million tons between 1963 and 1971; in Britain in 1972 freight carried on all inland waterways came to only 30 million tons, and was declining. An American conference of civil engineers recently estimated that one dollar will move one ton of cargo five miles by air, 15 miles by truck, 67 miles by rail and 335 miles by water. Systems such as container handling and LASH (Lighter Aboard Ship; see page 35) would make canals compatible with other methods of shipping.

was built in 1846 at the instigation of King Ludwig of Bavaria with 100 locks to carry it over the Rhine-Danube watershed. It could only pass 130 ton barges so that, although it survived into the 1940s, it needed too much labour to compete in the modern world and it is now being replaced by a new waterway.

In England the only equivalent of these great waterways is the Manchester Ship Canal, which is 36 miles (58 km) long with five locks. It was opened in 1894 to enable sea going ships of up to 4500 tons gross to reach the new port of Manchester.

In North America an outstandingly successful inland waterway was the famous Erie Canal built by the State of New York between 1817 and 1825 to link the Hudson River with Lake Erie. With 82 locks in a course of 363 miles (584 km) it was the longest canal in the world at the time of its opening. It was widened and deepened throughout as traffic grew until, in 1918, it was replaced by the New York State Barge Canal which can accommodate 2500 ton craft. North of this is the new (1959) St Lawrence Seaway, part canal, part river, which enables seagoing vessels to travel from Montreal to Lake Ontario and from there via the Welland Canal into Lake Erie.

All the other canals in eastern North America have fallen into disuse, but there is the great network of 6000 miles (10,000 km) of inland waterways formed by the Mississippi, its canalized tributaries and their associated canals. These have a common depth of 9 feet (3 m) and the smallest locks measure 600 by 100 ft (180 by 30 m). In the Southern states and connected with the Mississippi system are the Intracoastal waterways. Lock-free and a mixture of natural channels and artificial canals, they provide waterways for big barges sheltered from the sea. The Gulf Intracoastal runs for over 1000 miles (1600 km) from near the Mexican border to Florida where it is extended by the Atlantic Intracoastal as far as Norfolk, Virginia.

Compared with Brindley's little 70 feet (21 m) by 7 feet (2.1 m) locks with an average fall of 8 feet (2.4 m), some modern locks are of immense size. The largest in length and breadth is at Ijmuiden on the North Sea Ship Canal in Holland, which measures 1320 by 165 ft (402 by 50 m). The lock with the greatest fall is claimed by Russia with 138 feet (42 m) for a lock on the Irtish river navigation, though the 113 ft (34 m) deep John Day lock on the Columbia River section of the Mississippi system does not lag very far behind.

All these large locks are either on, or connected to, large river systems so that water supply problems do not occur. But even on summit level canals the availability of water no longer governs the size of locks as

Above: when the booster rockets for the Apollo space mission had to be transported the most convenient way was the Gulf Intercoastal waterway system.
Left: the Montech waterslope in France. A pool of water is pushed up the slope by locomotives pushing the dam.

Below: the Corinth canal saves a considerable trip around the Peloponnesus in Greece. It was blasted out of solid rock in the late 19th century.

brought into commission at Montech in southern France on the Garonne Lateral Canal. This consists of an inclined trough of concrete up which the barge, floating on a triangular wedge of water, is pushed by a moving concrete dam propelled by locomotives.

Sea canals

Another type of canal is the sea to sea ship canal designed to shorten a long sea passage. The trouble with this type of canal is that it is doomed to obsolescence because of the rapid increase in the size of shipping. Telford's Caledonian Canal was driven through the Great Glen of Scotland to enable sailing ships to avoid the long and perilous passage around Cape Wrath, but it was soon made obsolete by the coming of steam power and the increasing size of shipping. Telford was also responsible for the construction of the very similar Göta Canal in Sweden which opened an inland passage for Swedish shipping from the Baltic to the North Sea and so avoided the tolls levied by Denmark in the Kattegat. But here again, ships soon outgrew it.

The most famous 19th century canal builder was the Frenchman Ferdinand de Lesseps who was responsible for the Suez Canal. Because this 100 mile (160 km) long canal through the desert required no locks, its progressive enlargement has been relatively simple until its recent closure for political reasons.

De Lesseps also planned to drive a 50 mile (80 km) long lockless sea level canal through the Isthmus of Panama to unite the Atlantic with the Pacific. But although his army of workmen toiled from 1881 to 1889, the climate and the terrain defeated them. Malaria and yellow fever took a terrible toll of the work force and treacherous rock strata caused incessant slips in the vast cutting he planned through the spine of Panama. The present, locked, Panama Canal was built and opened by the Americans in 1914, but it is already becoming too small and too slow and there is talk of replacing it by a new lock-free canal such as de Lesseps dreamed of.

Construction of the first canal preceded that of the first railway by nearly 200 years, so canals are among the oldest works of civil engineering. Until the first 'steam navvies' (mechanical excavators) appeared in the 1870s, all canals were dug by hand and their beds made waterproof by a layer of clay, well trodden down. Modern canals may be lined with concrete.

Since the earliest days canals have seen a variety of methods of propulsion: sail, towage, first by men or horses and later by steam tugs or tractors hauling from the towpath. But nowadays the diesel engine has made the self-propelled barge almost ubiquitous. The penalty for this is that the banks of the modern canal have to be protected by interlocking piling against the erosion caused by the wash of passing traffic. Yet in terms of tonnage moved per horsepower expended, the canal still represents the cheapest from of inland transport devised by man.

was the case in Brindley's day. The modern canal engineer thinks in terms of pumping the lockage water back electrically rather than building costly dams to store more water at the summit level.

Boat lifts

Though water can be pumped back, a long flight of locks uses a great deal of another precious commodity —time. Hence from the earliest days engineers have schemed to save both water and time by substituting various forms of boat lift for lock flights. Of these the only one remaining in England is the Anderton Vertical lift of 1875, which lowers boats from the Trent and Mersey Canal to the River Weaver. Ironically, although this is the sole survivor in England and is no longer in commercial use, its English engineers went on to build four much larger lifts of similar type on the Canal du Centre in Belgium: these are still in use by 400 ton barges. Also in Belgium is the huge Ronquieres inclined plane lift on the Brussels-Charleroi Canal, which must be the largest canal structure in the world. It is a mile (1.6 km) long and lifts 1350 ton barges 220 feet (67 m). Another ingenious modern form of lift has just been

118

INDEX